# PASS THE POETRY, PLEASE!

# LEE BENNETT HOPKINS

# Pass the Poetry, Please!

## ⚜ THIRD EDITION ⚜

HarperCollins*Publishers*

# ACKNOWLEDGMENTS

Thanks are due to the following for the use of the copyrighted selections listed below:

Curtis Brown, Ltd., for permission to reprint "The Dance Has Ended." Copyright © 1980 by Lee Bennett Hopkins; "Good Books, Good Times!" Copyright © 1985 by Lee Bennett Hopkins.

Alfred A. Knopf, Inc., for "Dreams" from *The Dream Keeper and Other Poems* by Langston Hughes. Copyright © 1932 by Alfred A. Knopf, Inc., and renewed 1960 by Langston Hughes. Reprinted by permission of the publisher.

Library of Congress Cataloging-in-Publication Data
Hopkins, Lee Bennett.
  Pass the poetry, please! / Lee Bennett Hopkins. — 3rd ed.
    p.    cm.
  Includes bibliographical references and index.
  ISBN 0-06-027746-7. — ISBN 0-06-446199-8 (pbk.)
  1. Poetry—Study and teaching (Elementary)  2. Poetry—Authorship—Study and teaching (Elementary)  3. Education, Elementary—Activity programs.  4. Interdisciplinary approach in education.  I. Title.
LB1576.H64   1998                                                          98-19617
372.64—dc21                                                                    CIP

Typography by Christine Kettner
1  2  3  4  5  6  7  8  9  10
❖
Revised, Enlarged, and Updated Edition

*To my Poet-friends*
*who make it all possible.*
—L.B.H.

# CONTENTS

# PREFACE

First published in 1972, and reissued in a second edition in 1987, *Pass the Poetry, Please!* has been in print more than twenty-five years. This third edition has been reorganized, enlarged, and updated in terms of important happenings that have occurred in the world of poetry for children since 1987.

It is my firm belief that poetry can and must be an integral part of the total school curriculum, interwoven within every subject area.

My aim in this edition is to create a volume to serve as a practical reference for students coming into the teaching profession, for experienced teachers and librarians to keep abreast of the ever-widening genre, and for parents to bring poetry to their children.

*Pass the Poetry, Please!* contains four sections: Part One places the genre in current history and discusses the importance of how poetry should be presented to children; Part Two contains twenty-four interviews and biographical sketches of past masters as well as contemporary poets writing for children today; Part Three places emphasis on unleashing children's talents to create verse of their own; Part Four suggests dozens of tried-and-tested activities to integrate poetry into all areas of the elementary curriculum to enable students to experience the genre as a total entity rather than an isolated area of literature.

Over the years I have received generous help in preparing the first and second editions of *Pass the Poetry, Please!*, as

I have in readying this third edition. I thank the following, to whom I am greatly indebted: Mary L. Allison, who first believed in the book decades ago; Misha Arenstein, who listened for long, long hours; Charles J. Egita, whose patience never ceased; Bill Morris, Sally Doherty, and Anne Hoppe, incredible talents at HarperCollins; the many individuals in the publishing industry who share so much; Marilyn E. Marlow, for being my sage. A heartfelt thanks is especially given to Ann Tobias, my editor of this edition, who wisely told me, "When you climb the mountain, write about the mountain!" Due to her wisdom, I climbed.

Lee Bennett Hopkins
Scarborough, New York

# PASS THE POETRY, PLEASE!

# PART ONE

# "Poetry Refreshes the World"

Although poetry for children has long been an integral part of literature, the genre did not reach national recognition until 1977. At that time the National Council of Teachers of English (NCTE) established the country's first award for poetry—the NCTE Award for Excellence in Poetry for Children—presented annually to a living American poet for an aggregate body of work. Since 1982 the award has been given every three years. To date, the following poets have received this prestigious honor: David McCord (1977), Aileen Fisher (1978), Karla Kuskin (1979), Myra Cohn Livingston (1980), Eve Merriam (1981), John Ciardi (1982), Lilian Moore (1985), Arnold Adoff (1988), Valerie Worth (1991), Barbara Juster Esbensen (1994), and Eloise Greenfield (1997).

Books by these poets carry a seal designed by Karla Kuskin:

A sampling of the first ten winners' work is gathered in *A Jar of Tiny Stars*, edited by Bernice E. Cullinan.

The 1980s brought additional new beginnings for poetry for children. In 1982, for the first time in its history, the John Newbery Medal was awarded to a collection of original verse—Nancy Willard's *A Visit to William Blake's Inn*. The volume was also named a Caldecott Honor Book for its illustrations by Alice and Martin Provenson. The Newbery Medal, given annually since 1922 to the author of the most distinguished contribution to American literature for children published in the United States, and the Randolph Caldecott Medal, given annually since 1938 to the illustrator of the most distinguished picture book for children published in the United States, both administered by the American Library Association, are the most prestigious prizes awarded in the field of children's literature.

Another first for verse came in 1981, when *A Light in the Attic* by the popular poet Shel Silverstein reached number one on *The New York Times'* adult best-seller list and remained on the list for over three years.

In 1982, when the Broadway musical *Cats* (which is based on T. S. Eliot's *Old Possum's Book of Practical Cats*) opened at the Winter Garden Theatre in New York City, sales of the book began to soar, reaching more readers than it had since it was first published in 1939. Like *Cats'* legendary motto, "Now and Forever," Eliot's book continues to attract new generations of readers.

In 1989 *Joyful Noise* by Paul Fleischman became the second volume of poetry to receive the Newbery Medal.

In the early to mid-1990s I founded two additional poetry awards.

The Lee Bennett Hopkins Poetry Award is currently presented annually by The Children's Literature Council of Pennsylvania. It recognizes the work of an American poet or anthologist and is given for a volume of poetry, whether a single poem, an original collection, or an anthology. To date, the following books have received this award: *Sing to the Sun* by Ashley Bryan (1993), *Spirit Walker* by Nancy Wood (1994), *Beast Feast* by Douglas Florian (1995), *Dance With Me* by Barbara Juster Esbensen (1996), *Voices from the Wild* by David Bouchard, (1997), and *The Great Frog Race and Other Poems* by Kristine O'Connell George (1998).

The award includes a cash prize and a medallion featuring artwork by Jessie Willcox Smith, a Pennsylvania-born illustrator. As of 1999 the award will be presented by Penn State University.

The Lee Bennett Hopkins/International Reading Association (IRA) Promising Poet Award is given every three years to a poet who has published no more than two books of children's poetry. The goal of this award is to recognize and promote promising new poets who create verse for children. The first award was given in 1995, to Deborah Chandra for her two collections, *Balloons* and *Rich Lizard*. In 1998 it was presented to Kristine O'Connell George for *The Great Frog Race and Other Poems*. The award includes a cash prize.

The first National Poetry Month was declared in April 1994 by the Academy of American Poets. It was proposed in order to raise the general awareness of poetry across the nation, bringing poetry to the general public. And it worked! During the first few years National Poetry Month celebrated adult verse. Now that National Poetry Month is an established celebration, poetry for children has become a major thrust of the event in schools, libraries, and bookstores across the United States.

Poetry for children continues to gain in popularity. Thank goodness for this trend, for poetry must flow freely in our children's lives; it should come to them as naturally as breathing, for nothing—*no thing*—can ring and reverberate through hearts and minds as does poetry.

Poetry works with any grade, any age level. It meets the interests and abilities of anyone, anywhere, from the most gifted to the most reluctant reader; it opens a world of feelings for children they never thought possible; it is a source of love and hope that children carry with them the rest of their lives.

Children are natural poets. Visit a school playground or park on a spring day, and you see youngsters "rhyming." Three children playing jump rope might be exclaiming:

*Cinderella dressed in red*
*Went downstairs to bake some bread.*
*How many loaves did she bake?*
*One, two, three, four . . .*

until one misses and either this rhyme or another is re-cited for the next jumper. Another group of children beginning a game of hide-and-go-seek or tag may be deciding who is going to be "it" by chanting:

*Eenie, meenie, minee, mo,*
*Catch a tiger by the toe.*
*If it hollers, let it go,*
*Eenie, meenie, minee, mo.*

Or:

*My mother and your mother were hanging out clothes.*
*My mother punched your mother right in the nose.*
*What color blood came out?*
*R-E-D spells red and O-U-T spells out.*

Still other groups of girls and boys will be bouncing balls, calling out:

*A sailing sailor*
*Went to sea*
*To see what he could see, see, see.*
*And all that he could see, see, see*
*Was the sea, the sea,*
*The sea, sea, sea.*

Children make up their own nonsense rhymes, too:

*Booba, booba, baba, baba,*
*Twee, twee, toe, toe.*
*I know! I know!*

Rhyme is very present in the child's world.

For close to four decades, during which poetry has been a major factor in my work as a teacher, consultant, author, and anthologist, I have listened long and hard to girls and boys. I have encountered thousands of children across the United States and Canada in a variety of formal and informal settings. I have seen children in the early grades naturally "ooh" and "ah" when they heard a poem they liked; I have also seen them wince and screw up their faces when a poem did not please them.

In upper grades poetry serves as an excellent stimulus to better reading and nurtures a love of words. I use poetry with slow readers, those who cannot possibly get through a long story or novel but who can understand

and relish the message a poem conveys. Poems, being short, are not demanding or frustrating to these readers. They can start them, finish them, and gain from them without experiencing any discomfort whatsoever.

Many children in upper grades, whether slow readers or very good ones, many not be mature enough to tackle the sophisticated prose of some of America's men and women of letters. However, they can dip into poetry; they can easily read and understand poems by such masters as Emily Dickinson, Robert Frost, Langston Hughes, and Carl Sandburg. Thus, children's literary horizons can be extended through verses created by the finest of writers.

Poetry is so many things to so many people. There are as many definitions of poetry as there are poets; their work reflects this diversity, enabling us to choose from a myriad of poems. The anthologist Gerald D. McDonald stated in the preface to his collection *A Way of Knowing*:

> *Poetry can be wittier and funnier than any kind of writing; it can tell us about the world through words we can't forget; it can be tough or it can be tender; it can be fat or lean; it can preach a short sermon or give us a long thought (the shorter the poem sometimes, the longer the thought). And it does all this through the music of words.*

A poem is often an experience—something that has happened to a person, something that may seem very obvious, an everyday occurrence that has been set down in a minimum number of words and lines as it has never been set down before. These experiences depend upon the poets—who they are, when and where they live, why and how a specific thing affected them at a given moment.

Life has produced poets who need the quiet of the country, and they share what their senses reveal. For many the sight of a brook, a reflection in a pond, or the smell of newly mown hay inspires fresh images of nature. For others it is the excitement of city sidewalks, an image of a fire hydrant, or the city sounds and noises heard that spark verse.

Life itself is embodied in poetry, and each poem reveals a bit of life. Good poems make us say, "Yes, that's just how it is." Or, as Carl Sandburg wrote in his "Tentative (First Models) Definition of Poetry," thirty-eight gems printed as the preface to one of his longest poems, *Good Morning, America*: "Poetry is a series of explanations of life, falling off into horizons too swift for explanations."

There is really little difference between good poetry for children and good poetry for adults. Like poetry for adults, poetry for children must appeal to its audience and meet emotional needs and interests. We can read about what poetry or a poem *is*, what it *should* do, learn all about meters, rhyme schemes, cadence, and balance; yet all this does not necessarily help to make a poem meaningful. The one criterion we must set for ourselves as adults when choosing poems we are going to share with children is that we *love* the poems. If we don't like a particular poem, we shouldn't read it to our children; our distaste will certainly be obvious to them. There are plenty of poems around. Why bother with those that are not pleasing to us?

One day, while searching through my files of letters for a good definition of poetry, I found a brief message written by a young girl telling me how much she loved poetry; the letter ended with a P.S.: "A poem refreshes the world." How this simple definition impressed me. Poetry, indeed, "refreshes the world." Poetry can, and does, refresh the sometimes tumultuous world of childhood. I *know* this!

Many classroom teachers and parents may not want to read "sophisticated" poetry to children, particularly if the poetry by such greats as e. e. cummings, Theodore Roethke, or Wallace Stevens seems somewhat difficult. Some adults may never feel comfortable reading to children of primary- or even upper-grade ages such selections as T. S. Eliot's "The Naming of Cats" from *Old Possum's Book of Practical Cats*. This verse does have difficult pacing and hard-to-read phrases such as ". . . rapt contemplation" and "ineffable, effable/Effanineffable/Deep and inscrutable singular Name." Many children, however, relish the challenge presented by Eliot's richness of language and wordplay.

Karla Kuskin's experience as a child illustrates this impact. She states in "Profile: Karla Kuskin" by Alvina

Treut Burrows (*Language Arts*, November/December 1979): "There are lines in 'The Night Before Christmas' that will stay in my head forever because when I first learned the poem, I didn't understand all the words:

*"As dry leaves that before the wild hurricane fly,*
  *When they meet with an obstacle, mount to the sky,*
  *So up to the housetop the coursers they flew,*
  *With a sleigh full of toys, and St. Nicholas, too.*

I didn't know *hurricane*. I didn't know *obstacle*. I didn't know *coursers*; but I just loved the way they sounded."

Bringing children and poetry together can be one of the most exciting experiences in parenting or teaching. Over the years, however, I have noted in too many cases what I have coined the DAM approach—Dissecting, Analyzing, and *meaninglessly* Memorizing poetry to death.

Lee Shapiro, a first-year student teacher in a graduate class I taught in children's literature and storytelling at the City College of New York, wrote to me:

*I have felt for a long time that the structured introduction to poetry which I received in public and high school was frustrating and restricting besides being very painful. Being forced to dissect, analyze, and memorize poetry did not leave me much room for enjoyment. Until very recently I have avoided any kind of poetry. Now I have begun to explore on my own with great satisfaction the world of poetry. How much I missed!*

I well remember hating Shakespeare as a high school student. I was forced to dissect, analyze, and memorize some fifteen isolated lines from *Julius Caesar*. I received an A on the oral but a C on the written test because I misspelled several words and left out some punctuation marks! The next semester I suffered through a similar experience with Alfred Noyes' "The Highwayman." I, too, soon came to detest the sound of the word *poetry*! It was not something to be enjoyed—it was a test of endurance and my ability to memorize.

Looking back on those days, I laugh, but I still wonder why any student has to suffer through poetry presented in such a dreary, uninteresting fashion. I cannot even remember poems I *myself* wrote and wouldn't attempt reciting them without the printed words in front of me.

Even seasoned educators have to come to view poetry in a new light. M. Jerry Weiss, Distinguished Service Professor Emeritus of Communication at Jersey City State College in New Jersey, wrote in *The ALAN Review* (Winter 1997), after receiving a host of poetry volumes to review:

> *I have come to realize that my education to become an English teacher did not place enough emphasis on poets and poetry. While I read many classics, I had no idea of how rich the twentieth-century literature is with poetry. I needed to have spent less time worrying about*

*rhyme and meter. I was scanning when I should have been thinking about the not-so-fragile notions reflected in poems. I needed to listen to different drums, hear different sounds. Now I listen to the music. I am dancing, body and soul.*

As a young reader I wanted adventure, mystery, murder, passion. It wasn't until my adult years that I realized that Shakespeare and Noyes could have given me what I wanted then. Certainly the tragedies of Shakespeare dealt more passionately and romantically with life than did the drugstore magazines I bought with my weekly allowance. But I wasn't aware of this due to my soured poetic experiences.

In his acceptance speech on receiving the NCTE Award for Excellence in Poetry for Children, John Ciardi remarked:

*You can't say, "Memorize . . . and give it back on demand. . . ." You are the ones who must entice the student. If a student can be brought to say, "Wow!" to one poem, he or she can say "Wow!" to another. . . . Unless you and others like you can lead your students to this contact, Pac-Man is going to eat us all!*

Unfortunately there is a steady stream of curriculum guides that advocate dissecting poems to the point of the ridiculous. I share a personal experience: In 1980 I wrote "The Dance Has Ended," which reads in its entirety:

*Thirteen raindrops fell*
*signaling the beginning*
*of the dance's end.*

This haiku was created for a picture-book anthology I had compiled, *Elves, Fairies & Gnomes*, specifically to bridge a sequence of poems and pictures. It worked there. Isolated from the whole, it has little meaning. Many years later the piece was reprinted in a third-grade volume of a major textbook series; with it came a Teachers' Guide featuring Objectives, Summary for the Teacher, Pre-Reading, Post-Reading, and Enrichment.

Among the "Enrichment" activities is the following: "From the title of the poem what do you expect it to be about? . . . Why must the dance eventually end? . . . Identify the syllables in each word and ask students to judge whether or not each response is appropriate to the haiku structure. . . . Arrange a demonstration of origami, the traditional Japanese art of folding paper to form flowers, birds, fish, or other natural objects. . . ." And it went on—and on!

In another teaching guide the poem "City" from Langston Hughes' *The Collected Poems of Langston Hughes* is reprinted. The poem, a mere eight lines, beautifully describes a city waking up and going to bed. The guide suggests that after reading the poem aloud to children:

*Ask: What is a city? Name some cities. How does a city*
*spread its wings? What does the poet mean when he says,*

*"making a song in stone that sings"? How can a city go to bed? How can a city hang lights? Where would a city's head be?*

Really!

In the time—the meaningless time—students spend doing all this, they could relish an entire volume of poetry, coming away with so much more than a folded origami fish.

Even Mother Goose characters are being analyzed beyond belief. It is bad enough that poor Humpty Dumpty suffers a short demise via the rhyme written about him, but consider the following excerpt from an endless guide that appears in a major teachers' edition:

*Look at the chalkboard while I write the letter that starts with Humpty's name. . . . We use a capital H because it begins his name. There are other words in the rhyme that are not names. . . . They begin with a small h. They are* horses *and* had. *Listen to the words that follow. Tell me if they begin with the same sound as* Humpty. *[Recite* horses, head, happy. *Pause for their responses.] Now say after me:* Humpty, horses, head, happy. *[Write* Humpty, horses, head, happy *on the chalkboard. Direct the students to these four written words.] What letter do you see that is the same? [After their response underline the letter* h. . . . *Ask a variety of questions to help the students identify with the element.]*

The *element?* After such nonsensical interrogation, billed in both guides as "appreciation lessons," it would take a miracle or child masochist to ever ask for these, or any other poems, again.

A major teachers' magazine reprinted Karla Kuskin's delightfully witty verse "The Meal" from her book *Alexander Soames: His Poems* (reprinted in her *Dogs & Dragons, Trees & Dreams*), a romp about Timothy Tompkins whose breakfast consists of foodstuffs such as turnips, tea, onions, two cups of ketchup, a prune, and a pickle. But it isn't enough that children should delight in, laugh, sense the ironic humor, *love* the verse, or even be encouraged to seek other works by the poet. No! With the poem came a "reproducible ditto" encouraging students to "Help Timothy plan a better breakfast tomorrow morning. . . . Now create a menu to help Timothy plan nutritious breakfasts for the rest of the week. . . . Be sure to include things from all four food groups for each meal." Additional "creative activities" were offered. Poor Timothy! If I were he, I'd stick to a better breakfast and never, *ever* tell any teacher what I had consumed during my "pre-morning school activities."

Imagine working with a group of adults, asking each to read a recent popular novel, and then spend days, weeks, and months filling in work sheets, drilling on plot, characterization, meaning, and finishing with a multiple-choice test to assess their retention of the material. The adult reader would never pick up a book again.

Why then should our children be subjected to this kind of activity?

Long before they enter school, long before they can read a printed word, children are heard chanting familiar Mother Goose rhymes—verses passed down through centuries. Young children voluntarily reciting Mother Goose melodies do not stop to ponder over the meanings of words unfamiliar to them. They do not know, and may never know, what *curds* and *whey* are; nor do they know or care about the hidden personages behind peculiar names such as Wee Willie Winkie, Little Bo Peep, or the Queen of Hearts. To acquaint very young children with the fact that Mother Goose rhymes were reputedly political lampoons or satires about such historical figures as Mary Tudor, Henry VIII, or Mary, Queen of Scots, would be ludicrous. None of this matters. Children are in love with the easy rhymes, the alliteration, the quick action, and the humor that Mother Goose conveys.

I am often asked, "How do you read a poem aloud to children?" There is no trickery involved in reading poetry aloud. When a poem is read aloud with sincerity, boys and girls will enjoy its rhythm, its music, and will understand the work on their own level.

The guidelines below can help those who get butterflies in their stomachs when it comes to presenting poetry. These same points can be shared with children, for they, too, should be reading and sharing poetry aloud.

**1**. Before reading a poem aloud to an audience, read it aloud to yourself several times to get the feel of the words and rhythm. Know the poem well. Mark the words and phrases you want to emphasize, then read it exactly as you feel it.

**2**. Follow the rhythm of the poem, reading it naturally. The physical appearance of most poems on the printed page dictates the rhythm and mood of the words. Some poems are meant to be read softly, slowly, others at a more rapid pace.

**3**. Make pauses that please you—pauses that make sense. Some poems sound better when the lines are rhythmically strung together. Sometimes great effects can be obtained by pausing at the end of each line. Many of the poems by e. e. cummings and William Carlos Williams convey greater mood when they are read by pausing at the end of each short line, as though you were saying something to yourself for the first time, thinking of the word or words that will come from your tongue next. Isn't this how we speak? We think as we talk. Sometimes words flow easily— other times—

*they*
*come*
*slowly,*

*thinking-ly*
*from our*
*mouths.*

4. When reading a poem aloud, speak in a natural voice. Don't change to a high-pitched or bass-pitched tone. Read a poem as if you were telling children about a new car, or a television program you saw last night. Again, be sincere. A poem must interest you as well as be one that you feel is right for your audience.

5. After a poem is read, be quiet. Don't feel trapped into asking children questions such as "Did you like it?" Most girls and boys will answer yes—even if they didn't like it—because *you* selected and read it. And what if they didn't like it? By the time you begin finding out the reasons, the poem is destroyed and half of the class will see why they, too, shouldn't like it anymore.

Children sometimes find poetry distasteful when it is taught or presented via a one-week, once-a-year unit approach. But poetry is appropriate every day, all year long. There are many places within the day when a poem fits snugly. After all, poetry is not the exclusive property of the language arts. Why not open or close your next mathematics lesson with poems such as "One to Ten" by Janet S. Wong, or "Counting Birds" by Felice Holman, both in *Marvelous Math*, which I compiled? Or enhance a spelling lesson with David McCord's "You Mustn't Call It Hopsichord," "Spelling Bee," and "The Likes and Looks of Letters," all in *One at a Time*. The unit approach is good for social studies, science, and mathematics—but not for poetry!

We must do all we can to preserve and nurture the love of rhyme and rhythm, and the feeling for words, that young children have in them. They hear jingles on television daily; radios and cassette players blare tunes that either parents, peers, or older siblings play incessantly. As with Mother Goose rhymes, four-year-olds can sing lyrics to a popular song without *ever* seeing the words in print. They learn the words by repetition and love of a particular word scheme. And ask the average ten-, eleven-, twelve-year-old, or teenager how many popular songs he or she knows! Young people are entranced, almost mesmerized by their personal poets—today's songwriters. It should be an easy matter to channel some of that enthusiasm for songs into enthusiasm for poems.

What is poetry?

Does it really matter what poetry *is*?

It does matter, however, what it should evoke in each and every one of us.

What is poetry?

What is poetry to *you*?

When you find it, when you come across the something that makes you say, "I can *see* it! I can *hear* it!"—

and when you know that neither *you* nor your *children* may ever seem the same again—you will have found out what poetry truly is.

## REFERENCES

Bouchard, David. *Voices from the Wild: An Animal Sensagoria*. Illustrated by Ron Parker. Chronicle, 1996.

Bryan, Ashley. *Sing to the Sun*. Harper, 1992; also in paperback.

Chandra, Deborah. *Balloons and Other Poems*. Illustrated by Leslie Bowman. Farrar, Straus, 1990; also in paperback.

——. *Rich Lizard: And Other Poems*. Illustrated by Leslie Bowman. Farrar, Straus, 1993; also in paperback.

Cullinan, Bernice E., editor. *A Jar of Tiny Stars: Poems by NCTE Award-Winning Poets*. Illustrated by Andi MacLeod. Boyds Mills, 1996.

Eliot, T. S. *Old Possum's Book of Practical Cats*. Illustrated by Edward Gorey. New edition, Harcourt, 1982; also in paperback.

Esbensen, Barbara Juster. *Dance With Me*. Illustrated by Megan Lloyd. Harper, 1995.

Fleischman, Paul. *Joyful Noise: Poems for Two Voices*. Illustrated by Eric Beddows. Harper, 1988; also in paperback.

Florian, Douglas. *Beast Feast. Harcourt*, 1994.

George, Kristine O'Connell. *The Great Frog Race And Other Poems*. Illustrated by Kate Kiesler. Clarion, 1997; also in paperback.

Hopkins, Lee Bennett, editor. *Elves, Fairies & Gnomes: Poems*. Illustrated by Rosekrans Hoffman. Knopf, 1980.

———. *Marvelous Math*. Illustrated by Karen Barbour. Simon & Schuster, 1997.

Hughes, Langston. *The Collected Poems of Langston Hughes*. Edited by Arnold Rampersad. Knopf, 1994.

Kuskin, Karla. *Alexander Soames: His Poems*. Harper, 1962.

———. *Dogs & Dragons, Trees & Dreams*. Harper, 1980.

McCord, David. *One at a Time: His Collected Poems for the Young*. Illustrated by Henry B. Kane. Little, Brown, 1977.

McDonald, Gerald D., editor. *A Way of Knowing: A Collection of Poems for Boys*. Illustrated by Clare and John Ross. Crowell, 1959.

Sandburg, Carl. *Good Morning, America in The Complete Poems of Carl Sandburg*. Harcourt, 1970.

Silverstein, Shel. *A Light in the Attic*. Harper, 1981.

Willard, Nancy. *A Visit to William Blake's Inn: Poems for Innocent and Experienced Travelers*. Illustrated by Alice and Martin Provensen. Harcourt, 1981; also in paperback.

Wood, Nancy. *Spirit Walker*. Illustrated by Frank Howell. Doubleday, 1993.

# PART TWO

# From Adoff to Yolen

## ACQUAINTING
## CHILDREN WITH POETS

G iven guidance, children will come to know and love the rich variety of poetry written by past and contemporary poets.

In "The Cupboard Is Bare: The Need to Expand Poetry Collections," an article by Jeanne McLain and Lucille J. Lettow (*School Library Journal*, January 1987), the authors write:

> *As part of the study of poetry with children, the lives and contributions of individual poets should be explored. . . . By knowing more about poets, children will understand more about the nature of poetry. . . . Focusing on collections of a single poet's work . . . can provide new avenues for thought and new sources for unlimited experiences.*

I well agree!

Discussions of twenty-four American poets who have written volumes of original verse and whose works continue to be widely anthologized follow.

Direct quotations on the following pages stem either from my personal conversations and correspondence with the authors or from materials they have shared with me unless otherwise noted.

# ARNOLD ADOFF

*"... a fine poem*
*combines*
*the elements of*
*measuring music,*
*with a form like a*
*living frame*
*that holds*
*it all together."*

I MET ARNOLD ADOFF in 1967. Adoff and I shared similiar backgrounds. In the late 1950s and early 1960s he had been teaching in Harlem and on the Upper West Side of New York City. At that time I was working on a project sponsored by the Bank Street College of Education in five Harlem schools. We have been friends ever since.

Adoff began his professional journey into the world of poetry as an anthologist with the publication of *I Am the Darker Brother* in 1968. The volume grew out of the African-American poems he had been collecting to share with his students. In 1997 the book was reissued with a foreword by Nikki Giovanni, an introduction by Rudine Sims Bishop, and an afterword by Adoff tracing the nearly thirty-year span of this groundbreaking collection. Twenty-one new poems by nineteen poets were added, including such prominent voices as Rita Dove, Maya Angelou, and Ishmael Reed. The volume is indeed "an excellent gift to a new generation of readers," as Bishop states.

Adoff's career as a writer flourished after *Darker Brother*. In 1973, following the success of that book, he completed the comprehensive collection *The Poetry of Black America*, containing more than six hundred poems by over one hundred writers. He has created an astonishing body of work that includes prose, poetry, biography, and picture books.

"I have been a poet, deep inside, since I began writing as a teenager," he said. "By thirty, I was enough of a man to start to put things together and realize where the thrust should be directed. I wanted to influence the kids coming up. I wanted to anthologize adult literature of the highest literary quality and get it into classrooms and libraries for children and young adults. From that time on I threw myself full-force into creating books for children."

In 1969 he, his wife (the writer Virginia Hamilton), and their two children, Leigh Hamilton and Jaime Levi, left New York City to settle in Yellow Springs, Ohio. They built a redwood house on the old family farm where Hamilton grew up.

Defining poetry, Mr. Adoff told me, "There are as many definitions of poetry as there are different kinds of poems, because a fine poem combines the elements of measuring music, with a form like a living frame that holds it all together. My own personal preference is the music first that must sing out to me from the words. How does it sing, sound—then how does it look? I really want a poem to sprout roses and spit bullets; this is the ideal combination, and it is a tough tightrope that takes the kind of control that comes only with years of work. My poems should be read three or four times—once for the meaning, once for the music, and once for how the music and meaning go together."

In "Profile: Arnold Adoff" by Mary Lou White (*Language Arts*, October 1988), he talks further about the development of his hallmark style.

"When I am drafting a poem, I visualize myself surfing—only I don't surf, but I'm kind of doing so on a word processor or on a sheet of paper. That's the way kids should be gliding into the process of revision—not sweating and grinding, attempting to find a word that rhymes at the end of a line that could be in any way close to what they *really* wanted to say. Why create more locks? Why create more prisons? Why not open up a few walls?"

Commenting on his childhood, he said, "I was influenced at an early age by the world—I wasn't just a kid from the Bronx. I grew up with wonderful children's poets—and Yiddish poets as well. With no television, it was a marvelous time for the imagination to grow.

"At eleven years old, in the sixth grade, I was a very serious young boy. I loved to express myself through writing. If I'd never published a single poem in my life, I think I would always have been a poet. I never wanted to follow rules. In poetry you must master the rules that have gone before, and then you make up your own rules. After that you are free to make or break them as you develop and change."

His tenacity paid off. His work is distinctive and diverse, ranging from such titles as *black is brown is tan*, a picture book about an interracial family; *All the Colors of the Race*, thirty-six stylistic works written from the point of view of a child who has an African-American mother and a white father; *Eats* and *Chocolate Dreams*, reflecting his passion for food and eating. Other volumes include *Make a Circle, Keep Us In*, celebrating the joys and tribulations of going through a day—from eating peanut butter to ripping a pair of new pants—and *In for Winter, Out for Spring*, poems told from the perspective of a young girl witnessing various aspects of the four seasons.

In 1988 he created *Flamboyan*, a book he describes as "poet's prose," about a girl born with hair the color of the flame-red blossoms of the flamboyan tree that grows outside her window. Adoff came across some of Karen Barbour's brightly colored paintings while he was writing the book and felt she would be the perfect artist to interpret the story. She agreed to do the illustrations, and the result was a unique collaboration of his prose and Barbour's radiant drawings.

Also in 1988 he received the National Council of Teachers of English (NCTE) Award for Excellence in Poetry for Children. Adoff's multitalents are demonstrated by the variety of books he penned in the late 1990s—*Street Music*, fifteen poems that capture varied people and rhythms of city life; *Slow Dance Heartbreak Blues*, a young-adult collection filled with emotion about teenage experiences; *Love Letters*, twenty poems each in the form of a letter.

Decades ago in an interview in *Top of the News* (January 1972), he was asked, "What advice do you have for future writers?" He answered: "You must learn to control: Yourself as a conscious individual; your craft, work habits, self-discipline; the very form of the poem or prose piece. You must believe you have the power. Always write, and study, with others and alone, the work of other writers that is relevant. Don't beat your head against doors. Use your fists!"

He *still* believes this!

ADOFF TITLES CITED

*All the Colors of the Race*. Illustrated by John Steptoe.
   Lothrop, 1982; also in paperback.
*black is brown is tan*. Illustrated by Emily Arnold McCully.
   Harper, 1973; also in paperback.

*Chocolate Dreams.* Illustrated by Turi MacCombie. Lothrop, 1989.

*Eats: Poems.* Illustrated by Susan Russo. Lothrop, 1979; also in paperback.

*Flamboyan.* Illustrated by Karen Barbour. Harcourt, 1988.

*I Am the Darker Brother: An Anthology of Modern Poems by Negro Americans.* Illustrated by Benny Andrews. Macmillan, 1968; revised edition titled *I Am the Darker Brother: An Anthology of Modern Poems by African Americans,* Simon & Schuster, 1997; also in paperback.

*In for Winter, Out for Spring.* Illustrated by Jerry Pinkney. Harcourt, 1991; also in paperback.

*Love Letters.* Illustrated by Lisa Desimini. Scholastic, 1997.

*Make a Circle, Keep Us In: Poems for a Good Day.* Illustrated by Ronald Himler. Delacorte, 1975.

*Poetry of Black America, The: Anthology of the 20th Century.* Introduction by Gwendolyn Brooks. Harper, 1973.

*Slow Dance Heartbreak Blues.* Illustrated by William Cotton. Lothrop, 1985.

*Street Music: City Poems.* Illustrated by Karen Barbour. Harper, 1995.

# HARRY BEHN

*"Almost*
*everyone*
*is as full*
*of words*
*waiting*
*to sing*
*as a forest*
*is full*
*of birds*
*before*
*sunrise."*

FOURTEEN YEARS after the author's death in 1973, over a half century since it was first published in *The Little Hill*, a handsome single-volume edition of Harry Behn's poem *Trees* appeared, beautifully illustrated and designed by James Endicott. One of thirty poems in *The Little Hill*, "Trees" is a prime example of the poet's mastery of the couplet form.

Born in McCabe, Arizona, on September 25, 1898, Behn had the kind of childhood most children today would envy and can only live vicariously via television programs or film.

"When I was a small boy in Territorial Arizona, in the town of Prescott, in the Bradshaw Mountains, all the boys I played with were influenced by the Native Americans who lived in wickiups on the reservation across Granite Creek."

From the Native Americans Behn learned about nature—plants and animals, weather and the seasons. He stalked antelope, stirred up quail that whickered and whirred among junipers on lava hills, climbed canyons dark and pungent with pines, and was chief of a "home-made tribe" who called themselves The Mount Vernon Alley Long Beargrass Tribe, named partly after the alley behind the street where most of the members lived and partly after a Yavapai boy, Charlie Long Beargrass.

Behn often visited Charlie at his camp, sat around the fire, and listened to Charlie's father telling ancient tales. Nothing meant more to him than the lore he learned as a child from these friends.

Upon graduating from high school, he lived one summer with the Blackfeet tribe in Montana, until his parents persuaded him to attend college. In 1922 he received a B.S. degree from Harvard University; the next year he went to Sweden as an American-Scandinavian Fellow; following this he became involved in the arts and media, founding and directing The Phoenix Little Theatre and founding and editing *The Arizona Quarterly.*

He also did a great deal of work in radio broadcasting and taught creative writing at the University of Arizona.

In 1937 he moved to Connecticut to write and travel. He and his wife, Alice, raised three children.

Behn was fifty years old before he began writing for children. It began one summer evening when his three-year-old daughter pointed to the stars and said, "Moon babies." The next day he wrote a poem for her and continued writing poetry for both children and adults throughout his life.

His first book of poems for children, *The Little Hill*, was written for his three children, Pamela, Prescott, and Peter. Other books include *All Kinds of Time*, an unusual poetic picture book about clocks, time, and the seasons, and *Windy Morning*, a small volume containing many poems about nature and the seasons.

For children in the middle grades, the poet translated Japanese haiku in *Cricket Songs* and *More Cricket Songs*, with accompanying pictures chosen from the works of Japanese masters.

*The Golden Hive*, for older readers, reflected his remembrance of his childhood, his deep sense of the American past, and his joy in nature.

He commented, "My first memory is of a profound and sunny peace, of leaves, birds, animals, changing seasons, spring to summer, summer to fall, fall to winter, and the wonder of being alive. Those are the mysteries I later tried to evoke in poems I wrote about my childhood, the imprints of stillness determining which haiku I chose to translate. . . . Like all aborigines, children are accustomed to thinking about the beginnings of things, the creation of beauty, the wisdom of plants and animals, of how alive everything is, like stars and wildflowers, and how wonderfully different people can be from each other."

An adult book, *Chrysalis*, expresses his views on writing and appreciating poetry.

*Crickets and Bullfrogs and Whispers of Thunder*, a volume I edited after his death, contains fifty poems from five of his earlier volumes—*The Little Hill*, *Windy Morning*, *The Golden Hive*, *The Wizard in the Well*, and *Chrysalis*.

About his work, Peter Roop in "Profile: Harry Behn" (*Language Arts*, January 1985) wrote: "Fortunately for us he had the ability to capture a few of life's elusive wonders and cage them on a page. Yet, like everything else that slips away when grasped, we can't squeeze these poems too tightly for they might escape. They are the breath beyond what it is."

## BEHN TITLES CITED

*All Kinds of Time*. Harcourt, 1950.
*Chrysalis: Concerning Children and Poetry*. Harcourt, 1968.
*Crickets and Bullfrogs and Whispers of Thunder: Poems and Pictures by Harry Behn*. Poems selected by Lee Bennett Hopkins. Harcourt, 1984.
*Cricket Songs: Japanese Haiku*. Harcourt, 1964.

*Golden Hive, The: Poems and Pictures.* Harcourt, 1966.

*Little Hill, The.* Harcourt, 1949.

*More Cricket Songs: Japanese Haiku.* Harcourt, 1971.

*Trees.* Illustrated by James Endicott. Henry Holt, 1992; also available in paperback.

*Windy Morning: Poems and Pictures.* Harcourt, 1953.

*Wizard in the Well, The: Poems and Pictures.* Harcourt, 1956.

# G W E N D O L Y N
# B R O O K S

*"Writing*

*is*

*a*

*delicious*

*agony."*

GWENDOLYN BROOKS was the first African American to win the Pulitzer Prize for Poetry. In 1950 it was awarded to her for a volume of adult poems, *Annie Allen*, which followed her successful *A Street in Bronzeville.*

She recalls the day a reporter from the Chicago *Sun Times* called her with the news that she had won the coveted award.

"I was stunned. I was getting ready to take my nine-year-old son, Henry, to the movies since I didn't want us to sit alone in the dark. We were very poor. Our lights had been turned off because we hadn't paid the bill. So we went to the movies, but I don't think I saw or heard a thing. I kept believing and not believing

I'd won the Pulitzer Prize!"

Since that historic moment Brooks has gone on to receive more than seventy honorary doctorate degrees and a host of awards.

Brooks was born in Topeka, Kansas, on June 7, 1917; since the age of one month she has lived in Chicago, Illinois. She was profoundly interested in poetry at a very early age. When she was thirteen years old, her poem "Eventide" appeared in a well-known magazine of the time, *American Childhood*. The pay was six copies of the issue! Despite the fact that between her sixteenth and seventeenth years she had close to one hundred poems published in *Chicago Defender*, the first black newspaper to enjoy national readership, it wasn't until she was twenty-eight years old that her work appeared in the prominent publication *Poetry: A Magazine of Verse*.

Most of her body of work is directed to mature students and adult readers. Through her poetry she speaks about the African-American experience in vivid, compassionate words.

Fortunately, Brooks wrote one volume of poems for young readers, *Bronzeville Boys and Girls*, a collection in which she set herself the task of writing "a poem a day in order to complete the book's deadline." Published in 1956 and still relevant today, the book presents poignant views of children living in the crowded conditions of an inner city in the United States. Each of the thirty-four poems bears the name of an individual child and is devoted to his or her thoughts, feelings, and emotions. There is "Val," who does not like the sound "when grownups at parties are laughing," and who would "rather be in the basement," or "rather be outside"; "Keziah," who has a secret place to go; "Pauline," who questions her mother's advice about growing up, asking, "What good is sun/if I can't run?"; and "Robert, Who Is a Stranger to Himself."

*Bronzeville Boys and Girls* is one book that should be in every library, available when you want and need it. And you will—time and time again.

Brooks's life story is chronicled in her *Report from Part One,* telling of her family background, childhood years, her "'prentice years," her marriage and children, her contacts with other African-American writers, and her journey to Africa.

In 1962 she was invited by President John F. Kennedy, along with other leading poets, to read at a poetry festival at the Library of Congress in Washington, D.C. There, just prior to his death, she met Robert Frost, who offered warm praise of her work. From 1985 to 1986 she served as Consultant in Poetry to the Library of Congress; in 1994, at the age of seventy-seven, she received the National Book Foundation's medal for Distinguished Contributions to American Literature.

On being a poet, she states: "I think a little more should be required of the poet than perhaps is required of the sculptor or the painter. The poet deals in words with which everyone is familiar. We all handle words. And I think the poet, if he or she wants to speak to anyone, is constrained to do something with those words so that they will 'mean something,' will *be* something that a reader may touch.

"I'm very pleased with the way my life turned out. Oh, it hasn't been all joys and roses and honey and cream. But I'm glad that I wanted to write, and I *did* write, and I'm glad I stuck with it. Writing is a delicious agony."

Mother of two grown children, Henry and Nora, Brooks stills works and lives on the South Side of Chicago.

## BROOKS TITLES CITED

*Annie Allen.* Harper, 1949; reissued by Greenwood, 1971.

*Bronzeville Boys and Girls.* Illustrated by Ronni Solbert. Harper, 1956.

*Report from Part One.* Prefaces by Don L. Lee and George Kent. Broadside, 1972.

*Street in Bronzeville, A.* Harper, 1945.

# JOHN CIARDI

*"Poetry*
*is*
*where*
*every*
*line*
*comes*
*to*
*rest*
*against*
*a*
*white*
*space. "*

IN THE LATE 1960s, before the light verse of Shel Silverstein and Jack Prelutsky was being collected in books, I met a man who created a body of work that rang with nonsense, echoed the serious, and delighted readers of all ages.

The man was John Ciardi.

Born in Boston, Massachusetts, on June 24, 1916, the only son of Italian immigrant parents, John Anthony

Ciardi grew up in Medford, Massachusetts. He began his higher education at Bates College in Lewiston, Maine, but transferred to Tufts University in Boston, receiving his B.A. in 1938. Then, winning a scholarship to the University of Michigan, he obtained his master's degree in 1939. His first book of adult poetry, *Homeward to America*, appeared in 1940.

"I always wanted to be a poet," Ciardi told me. "I took all sorts of courses in English in college and graduate school. John Holmes, a fine poet and my teacher at Tufts, persuaded me to take poetry seriously in my sophomore year. In graduate school Professor Roy Cowden gave me great help."

One of America's foremost contemporary poets, Ciardi, a translator of Dante's work, was an English professor at Kansas City University, Harvard, and Rutgers. After twenty years of teaching he resigned, becoming poetry editor of *The Saturday Review* from 1956 to 1972. He had also served as director of the Bread Loaf Writers' Conference at Middlebury College in Vermont, a group he was associated with for almost thirty years.

After successfully writing adult poetry for years, he decided to write for the children he was surrounded by.

"I wrote first for my sister's children, from about 1947 to 1953, when my wife, Judith, and I were living with them. Subsequently, I wrote for my own children as they came along, then for myself. My children, John Lyle Pritchard, Myra, and Benn Anthony, were in a hurry to grow up; I wasn't, so I wrote for my own childhood."

His first book of poetry for children, *The Reason for the Pelican*, appeared in 1959. In its review *The Horn Book* wrote "a warm and deserved welcome to this distinctive piece of publishing." *The New York Times* designated it as one of The Ten Best Children's Books of the Year.

A thirty-fifth-anniversary edition of the volume appeared in 1994, with new illustrations by Dominic Catalano and an afterword by X. J. Kennedy. In it Kennedy writes, "Ciardi threw open the musty old parlor of American children's verse, with its smell of rose petals and camphor, and he let in a blast of fresh air. . . . He altered the way we look at poetry for children, helping us see it as a fun-filled romp instead of a saccharin pill or a dose of propriety. . . ."

*The Reason for the Pelican* contains a range of poetry from "The Bugle-Billed Bazoo: The noisiest bird that ever grew . . . [who is] even noisier than YOU," to the beauty of nature in "How to Tell the Top of a Hill," and "The River Is a Piece of Sky," poems that continue to be anthologized over and over again. *The Reason for the Pelican* is one of the reasons *for* poetry. It should not be missed.

When asked how he approached his work, Ciardi replied that he had no system of writing. "It's like lazy fishing. Drop a line, sit easy. If a fish bites, play it, if not, enjoy the weather!"

Ciardi's favorite book, *I Met a Man*, a collection of

thirty-one poems, appeared in 1961. "It's my favorite because I wrote it on a first-grade vocabulary level when my daughter was in kindergarten. I wanted it to be the first book she read through, and she learned to read from it. Almost any child halfway through first grade should be able to read the first poems. Any bright child toward the end of first grade should be able to solve the slight added difficulties of the later poems."

Many of Ciardi's poems are spoofs of parent-child relationships. *The Monster Den*, subtitled *Or Look What Happened at My House—and to It*, was about his children. "It was a way of spoofing them. Kidding with love and some restraint can be a happy relationship. We were never a somber family."

Ciardi once remarked, "I have written some adult poems *about* children that are *not* for them. The closest I come to pointing out the difference between poetry for children versus poetry for adults is that children's poems are *eternal*; adult poems are *mortal*."

Two of his collections for children, *The Man Who Sang the Sillies* and *You Read to Me, I'll Read to You*, contain such "eternal" verses as "Some Cook!" and "Mummy Slept Late and Daddy Fixed Breakfast." *Doodle Soup* features thirty-eight mostly humorous verses with such titles as "The Dangers of Taking Baths," "The Best Part of Going Away Is Going Away from You," and "Why Pigs Cannot Write Poems."

After his death on March 30, 1986, two more volumes

of his work for children were published, *The Hopeful Trout and Other Limericks* and *Mummy Took Cooking Lessons*.

In the early 1990s Boyds Mills Press reissued his classic volumes *You Know Who* and *Someone Could Win a Polar Bear*, containing the original black-and-white illustrations by Edward Gorey.

In an article, "Profile: John Ciardi" (*Language Arts*, November/December 1982), Norine Odland wrote: "There is magic in the poetry John Ciardi has written for children. He uses words with whimsical agility. Humor in his poems allows a child to reach for new ways to view ordinary things and places in the world. In a few lines, a Ciardi poem can move a listener from one mood to another; the words tell the reader how the poem should be read."

Upon Ciardi's death, John Frederick Nims, a former *Poetry* magazine editor, stated: "I don't know of another poet who so completely put his life into poetry. I don't know of anyone who talked about poetry in a way that made more sense or put things more strikingly. . . . He was a very important influence on the poetry of our time."

For adult readers *The Selected Letters of John Ciardi*, edited by Edward Cifelli, provides 378 letters spanning his life from age nineteen until his death at sixty-seven, documenting correspondence he exchanged with such well-known writers as Isaac Asimov, Theodore Roethke, and Muriel Rukeyser. And *The Collected Poems of John*

*Ciardi*, also edited by Cifelli, contains 450 of the more than 700 poems Ciardi wrote during his lifetime.

In 1982, when he received the National Council of Teachers of English (NCTE) Award for Excellence in Poetry for Children, I had the privilege of attending a dinner party in his honor. During the evening he captivated the guests by reciting from memory a host of his incredible verses, work admired by critics and colleagues alike. How lucky I was to have met this man!

## CIARDI TITLES CITED

*Collected Poems of John Ciardi, The.* Compiled and edited by Edward Cifelli. University of Arkansas Press, 1997.

*Doodle Soup.* Illustrated by Merle Nacht. Houghton, 1985.

*Homeward to America.* Henry Holt, 1940.

*Hopeful Trout and Other Limericks, The.* Illustrated by Susan Meddaugh. Houghton, 1989.

*I Met a Man.* Illustrated by Robert Osborn. Houghton, 1961.

*Man Who Sang the Sillies, The.* Illustrated by Edward Gorey. Lippincott, 1961; also in paperback.

*Monster Den, The: Or Look What Happened at My House—And to It.* Illustrated by Edward Gorey. Lippincott, 1966; reissued by Boyds Mills, 1991.

*Mummy Took Cooking Lessons and Other Poems.* Illustrated by Merle Nacht. Houghton, 1990.

*Reason for the Pelican, The.* Illustrated by Madeline Gekieve. Lippincott, 1959; reissued by Boyds Mills, illustrated by Dominick Catalano, 1994.

*Selected Letters of John Ciardi, The.* Edited by Edward Cifelli. University of Arkansas Press, 1991.

*Someone Could Win a Polar Bear.* Illustrated by Edward Gorey. Lippincott, 1970; reissued by Boyds Mills, 1993.

*You Know Who.* Illustrated by Edward Gorey. Lippincott, 1964; reissued by Boyds Mills, 1991.

*You Read to Me, I'll Read to You.* Illustrated by Edward Gorey. Lippincott, 1962; also in paperback.

# LUCILLE CLIFTON

*"... lives
become
generations
made out of
pictures
and words
just kept."*

I N EARLY 1986 Myra Cohn Livingston and I proposed a program for the annual International Reading Association (IRA) convention to be held in Anaheim, California. We suggested staging a full day-and-a-half extravaganza on the state of poetry in the 1980s, and we invited X. J. Kennedy, Karla Kuskin, Charlotte Zolotow, and Lucille Clifton to participate.

The second I met Clifton, I felt sunshine glowing through the room. So did the packed audience; Clifton embraced everyone with the reading of her poems and her sage commentary on both life and a writing life. I feel the same way each and every time we meet. I knew then, at once, she was a *good* woman!

Clifton was born in Depew, New York, on June 27, 1936. Her father, Samuel, was a steelworker, her mother, Thelma, a launderer and homemaker. Her family roots are well detailed in her eloquent memoir *Generations*, a eulogy to her parents.

Reading and listening to her family tell stories and recite poetry was an important part of her childhood years. One of her favorite childhood memories was of discovering she could get a library card and go to a place where she could check out books for free.

School was also important to her. "I enjoyed school so much, I would have gone on weekends if they had let me," she said.

Always interested in poetry, Clifton had her first poetry appear in a literary magazine published by the University of Buffalo while she was a teenager.

After graduating from Fosdick Masten Park High School in Buffalo, New York, she attended Harvard University and, later, Fredonia State Teacher's College.

In 1969 the poet Robert Hayden submitted her poems for the Young Men's Hebrew Association Discovery Award. After she won the honor, her first book of adult poetry, *Good Times*, was published. In 1987 it was re-issued under the title *Good Woman* and included poems written between 1969 and 1980.

In the article "Profile: Lucille Clifton" by Rudine Sims (*Language Arts*, February 1982), Clifton was quoted as saying:

*I never thought about being a writer. I didn't know it was something you could do. I never heard of Gwen Brooks. The only writers I saw were the portraits they have in school. Like Longfellow . . . they were all bearded men— white, dead, old—and none of that applied to me. It was something that never occurred to me.*

In 1970 Clifton created the character Everett in *Some of the Days of Everett Anderson*, which she wrote because she "wanted to write something about a little boy who was like the boys my children might know, for my children and others."

This was the first in a series of books that tenderly portrayed the experiences of an African-American child living in Apartment 14A in an inner city. The universalities, however, that Clifton pens—being afraid, feeling lonely, and just wondering—echo many children's lives. The books are for all readers—everywhere.

Seven additional titles appeared featuring the delightful Everett, including *Everett Anderson's Goodbye*, a touching portrait of the young boy coming to grips with his father's death. In a sparse number of words we follow the child's struggle through the five stages of grief— denial, anger, bargaining, depression, and acceptance.

Clifton is the mother of six grown children— Frederica, Channing, Gillian, Graham, Alexia, and Sidney. "I had six kids in seven years," she said, "and when you have a lot of children, you tend to attract children, and you see so many kids, you get ideas from that. I have great respect for young people. I like them enormously."

She has received numerous honors for her writing; to date she is the only poet to have had two books named finalists for the Pulitzer Prize for Poetry in one year—*Good Woman* and *Next*.

With her usual wit she recalled an invitation she received to do a reading at the Library of Congress.

"The next day," she said, "I was ironing clothes and I said, 'What is this great *poet* doing ironing?' My kids laughed and said, 'Are you crazy?'—and I had to come back to earth!"

In recent years she has spent much of her time writing collections of poems for adults, among them *Quilting*, poems written between 1987 and 1990, *Next*, *The Book of Light*, and *The Terrible Stories*, volumes packed with powerful poetic pieces that can, and must, be shared with young-adult readers.

Don't miss viewing a wonderful one-hour videotape, *Lucille Clifton*. It was recorded in 1996 by Lannan Literary Videos—the year she received the Lannan Literary Award for Poetry presented by the Lannan Foundation in Los Angeles, California, an organization dedicated to supporting innovative and sometimes controversial forms of contemporary art and literature.

Viewers of the tape will experience this charming, witty, earthy, tough woman reading and commenting on twenty-two poems, discussing her life and her bout with cancer, and telling us how her "poems come out of wonder"—how, through poetry, we can try to understand the world. The last half of the tape features an interview conducted by the poet Quincy Troupe.

About her writing habits she said, "I write in spurts. I'm completely undisciplined. I never do all the things you're supposed to do, like write at the same time every day. And I can't write if it's quiet."

Gwendolyn Brooks tenderly describes Clifton as "a warmwisewoman. (It is necessary to close those words into one!) Her talent is inclusive . . . intuitive, *and* conducted . . . adventurous and unafraid."

At the end of Clifton's *Generations* she writes: "Things don't fall apart. Things hold. Lines connect in thin ways that last and last and lives become generations made out of pictures and words just kept. . . . Our lives are more than the days in them, our lives are our line and we go on."

Her lines will continue to go on—and on—warmwisewonderfully.

### CLIFTON TITLES CITED

*Book of Light, The.* Copper Canyon Press, 1993; also in paperback.

*Everett Anderson's Goodbye.* Illustrated by Ann Grifalconi. Holt, Rinehart, 1983.

*Generations: A Memoir.* Random House, 1976.

*Good Woman: Poems and a Memoir, 1969–1980.* BOA, 1987; also in paperback.

*Next: New Poems.* BOA, 1987; also in paperback.
*Quilting: Poems 1987–1990.* BOA, 1991; also in paperback.
*Some of the Days of Everett Anderson.* Illustrated by Evaline
    Ness. Holt, Rinehart, 1970; also in paperback.
*Terrible Stories, The: Poems.* BOA, 1996.

# BARBARA JUSTER ESBENSEN

*"A*

*poem*

*is*

*merely—*

*'A dance of breath*

*that has learned*

*to fly!'"*

BARBARA JUSTER ESBENSEN told me: "My favorite thing to tell children when I visit schools is that poets lie! But, of course, I quickly tell them *how* we lie! In the poem 'Performance' in *Dance With Me*, I use lines such as 'the trees lock crooked arms' and 'a breeze remembers how to rhyme.' Of course trees do *not* have arms to lock, and a breeze cannot remember. But poets have to be poetic. And we have to lie. Sometimes lying is just wonderful!"

*Dance With Me*, a book of fifteen poems depicting dance in nature, was the 1996 winner of the Lee Bennett Hopkins Poetry Award.

At breakfast the morning after a dazzling award

ceremony, Esbensen looked radiant, chatting about her career, bubbling with her endless enthusiasm. It was hard to imagine she would turn seventy-one years old in just a few weeks.

"Seventy-one!" she exclaimed. "You know what, Lee? I'm really eighteen or twenty. I'm still a schoolgirl. I'm in love with life."

Although we talked on the telephone many times after that meeting, it was the last time I saw her. On October 25, 1996, she died.

Her career was the stuff writers' dreams are made of.

Born in Madison, Wisconsin, on April 28, 1925, she spent the first twenty years of her life there. Both her father, who was a doctor, and her mother, a singer, encouraged her artistic talents from a very early age.

Her tenth-grade teacher, Eulalie Beffel, nurtured her poetic talent and was *the* influence on her development as a writer. Esbensen recalled putting a poem on Beffel's desk, a piece she wrote about Russia invading Finland. Beffel was thrilled with the work and told her, "You are a writer!"

"That did it," Esbensen said. "It was there and then I knew I *was* a writer."

Beffel introduced the class to works by Amy Lowell, Emily Dickinson, Stephen Vincent Benét, and others— poets who wrote free verse.

"I felt after reading these greats that I was going to faint and that I, too, could write without using rhyme.

Beffel changed my life and I never stopped being in touch with her. Until her death she saw every sentence, every paragraph, every poem I ever wrote. My first book of poems, *Swing Around the Sun*, is dedicated to my parents and Beffel."

Graduating from the University of Wisconsin with a major in art, Esbensen taught art in grades kindergarten through twelve. Upon moving to Eureka, California, she became a classroom teacher.

*Swing Around the Sun*, twenty-eight poems celebrating the seasons, was published in 1965. Her poems were composed day after day in the public library during a summer break from her third-grade teaching position.

In 1975 she wrote a professional book, *A Celebration of Bees*, based on her teaching strategies and philosophy of motivating children to write poetry. The book was a gem—one I used constantly in workshops long before I met Esbensen. Unfortunately, it went out of print. A new edition, however, appeared in 1995. Nikki Giovanni praised it, calling it "An insightful way of reaching that marvelous joyful core called 'creativity.' Good for children—and good for the child in us all."

Nineteen years after *Swing Around the Sun* appeared, she wrote a second book of poetry for children, *Cold Stars and Fireflies*. And then the poetry began to flow— *Words with Wrinkled Knees*, *Who Shrank My Grandmother's House?*, *Dance With Me*, and *Echoes for the Eye*—all written within a decade.

In between her books of verse, Esbensen created numerous books of nonfiction such as *Tiger With Wings: The Great Horned Owl*; *Baby Whales Drink Milk*; and retellings of Native American Ojibway tales, including *The Star Maiden* and *Ladder to the Sky*.

In "Profile: Barbara Juster Esbensen" (*Language Arts*, November 1994), M. Jean Greenlaw, who chaired the award committee, asked Esbensen how she felt upon receiving the National Council of Teachers of English (NCTE) Poetry Award for Excellence in Poetry for Children.

"I was astonished," she said, "because my experience has been that poetry is a little bit of a stepchild in the world of literature, and it is nice to know that somebody is reading it and considering it valuable. I think the award validates all the time that I have spent adoring words and putting them together and having a marvelous time looking at what is going on the page . . . so this is wonderful: It makes me feel like a star!"

After many years of moving around the country, while raising six children, Esbensen settled with her family in Edina, Minnesota, where her husband, Tory, served as assistant superintendent of the Edina schools until his retirement in 1980.

At the 1996 award ceremony for *Dance With Me*, in Hershey, Pennsylvania, Esbensen turned to me from the dais and said, "Lee, you can dance with me anytime."

I miss the dance steps but will forever hear the music—the music of her words.

## EBENSEN TITLES CITED

*Baby Whales Drink Milk.* Illustrated by Lambert Davis.
Harper, 1994; also in paperback.

*Celebration of Bees, A: Helping Children Write Poetry.*
Winston, 1975; revised edition, Holt, 1995.

*Cold Stars and Fireflies: Poems of the Four Seasons.* Illustrated
by Susan Bonner. Crowell, 1984.

*Dance With Me. Illustrated by Megan Lloyd. Harper,* 1995.

*Echoes for the Eye: Poems to Celebrate Patterns in
Nature.* Illustrated by Helen K. Davie. Harper, 1996.

*Ladder to the Sky: How the Gift of Healing Came to the
Ojibway Nation.* Illustrated by Helen K. Davie. Little,
Brown, 1989.

*Star Maiden, The: An Ojibway Tale.* Illustrated by Helen K.
Davie. Little, Brown, 1988; also in paperback.

*Swing Around the Sun.* Illustrated by Barbara Fumagalli.
Lerner, 1965.

*Tiger With Wings: The Great Horned Owl.* Illustrated by
Mary Barrett Brown. Orchard, 1991; also in paperback.

*Who Shrank My Grandmother's House?:* Poems of Discovery.
Illustrated by Eric Beddows. Harper, 1992.

*Words with Wrinkled Knees: Animal Poems.* Illustrated by
John Stadler. Harper, 1986; reissued by Boyds Mills,
1997.

# AILEEN FISHER

*"Poetry is*
*a rhythmical*
*piece of*
*writing*
*that leaves*
*the reader*
*feeling that*
*life is*
*richer*
*than*
*before."*

I served as chair of the National Council of Teachers of English (NCTE) Award for Excellence in Children's Poetry in 1978—the year Aileen Fisher became the second recipient. Although we had corresponded for many, many years before 1978, we had never met. Via telephone I tried hard to persuade her to attend the award ceremony in Kansas City, Missouri, in November. I well knew how she felt about traveling. Many times she expressed her feelings about leaving her home in Colorado.

"I like centrality in my life and peace and quiet, which means that I avoid commercialized excitement, cities, traffic, polluted air, noise, confusion, travel, crowds, and airports," she told me.

I still tried.

In March 1978 she wrote to me saying: "You sound very persuasive and I will . . . really think about attending. The promise that I can wear slacks makes it sound within a realm of possibility at least. I have never been able to make speeches. . . . I am sure all these people are very nice people individually and I know I'd like them. It's getting so many together in a bunch, Lee, that startles me."

I wasn't that "persuasive"! She did not come to Kansas City.

Years later, however, when NCTE met in Denver, Fisher did come to meet me. And what a meeting it was— a true thrill of my life.

Born on September 9, 1906, in Iron River, a small mining town in the Upper Peninsula of Michigan, near the Wisconsin border, Fisher tells about her early childhood years.

"Horse-and-buggy days were waning when I was born. There were still hitching posts and boardwalks along Main Street, but the Model T Ford was on its way, along with electric lights and bathrooms and crystal radio sets. I faced life in a changing world, as the second child of a middle-aged businessman and a young kindergarten teacher."

She studied at the University of Chicago for two years and then transferred to the School of Journalism at the University of Missouri. After receiving her degree in 1927, she worked in a little theater during the summer, then went back to Chicago to look for a job. She found one—as an assistant in a placement bureau for women journalists! That fall she sold her first poem, a nine-line verse entitled "Otherwise," to *Child Life* magazine.

Fisher continued writing poems for children while living and working for five more years in Chicago, saving her small salary and hoping to return to the country. In 1932 she left the city, an environment that even then she detested, and settled in Colorado. The following year her first collection of poetry, *The Coffee-Pot Face*, appeared; about half of the verses in it had previously been published in *Child Life*. The book became a Junior Literary Guild selection. Since that time Fisher has touched thousands upon thousands of children with her warm, wondrous writing.

Fisher described her work habits as always being methodical.

"I try to be at my desk four hours a day, from eight A.M. to noon. Ideas come to me out of experience and from reading and remembering. I usually do a first draft by hand. I can't imagine writing verse on a machine, and for years I wrote nothing but verse, so I formed the habit of thinking with a pencil or pen in my hand. I usually rework my material, sometimes more, sometimes less. I never try out my ideas on children, except on the child I used to know—*me*! Fortunately, I remember pretty well what I used to like to read, think about, and do. I find even today that if I write something I like, children are pretty apt to like it too. I guess what it amounts to is I never grew up.

"For my thirteenth birthday my mother planned a specially nice party. But I was devastated. 'I don't want a party,' I cried. 'I don't want to be thirteen. I don't want to grow up.'

"Well, over the years I have discovered that you don't really have to grow up. The outside world can keep changing for better or for worse. But you can still go barefoot in the grass, or lie on a pile of autumn leaves, or get up at five thirty in the morning to go walking with your dog."

Today Fisher lives in Boulder, Colorado, at the foot of Flagstaff Mountain. However, when she first went to Colorado, she lived on a ranch where "no electricity was available, so life was organized very well without it. When we could finally have it, we didn't want it!

"I'm not nor ever was a bit gadget-minded. My favorite possessions are books, and interesting pieces of Colorado wood from the timberline which have been enhanced by wood rasp, chisel, and some sandpaper. My pleasures in life are found through animals, especially dogs, mountain climbing, hiking, working with wood, unorthodox gardening, a few people in small doses, and reading. For me early morning on a mountain trail is the height of bliss."

Sadly, two collections of her poetry have gone out of print—*Out in the Dark and Daylight*, over 140 poems reflecting various moods of the four seasons, and *Always Wondering*, eighty-one of her personal favorite verses composed over many years. Both volumes are well worth looking for in libraries.

Happily, Fisher's poetry continues to be widely anthologized. What a treat it is for children to meet her via her work. *This* is the height of bliss.

## FISHER TITLES CITED

*Always Wondering: Some Favorite Poems of Aileen Fisher.*
Illustrated by Joan Sandin. Harper, 1991.
*Coffee-Pot Face, The.* McBride Company, 1933.
*Out in the Dark and Daylight.* Illustrated by Gail Owens.
Harper, 1980.

# ROBERT FROST

*"Like*
*a piece of*
*ice on a*
*hot stove*
*the poem*
*must ride on*
*its*
*own*
*melting."*

ROBERT LEE FROST, born in San Francisco, California, on March 26, 1874, did not attend school until he was twelve years old and didn't read a book until he was fourteen.

In *Interviews with Robert Frost* by Edwin Connery Lathem, a Frost scholar, the poet commented, ". . . After I had read my first book a new world opened up for me, and after that I devoured as many of them as I could lay my hands on. But by the time I was fifteen, I was already beginning to write verses."

In 1885, after his father's death, he moved with

his mother and sister to Lawrence, Massachusetts, his father's birthplace, where in 1890 Frost's first poem, "La Noche Triste," was published in the school paper. At graduation from Lawrence High School, he was co-valedictorian. The other student to win this honor, Elinor White, became his wife in 1895.

Frost attended Dartmouth College but left to teach in his mother's private school. From 1897 to 1899 he attended Harvard University, but he became ill and did not finish his education. After this, as he vacillated between teaching and dairy farming, he grew as a poet.

In 1912 Frost, with his wife and four children, moved to England feeling that if he broke away from New England life, he could concentrate on writing poetry. A year later his first book of adult poems, *A Boy's Will*— a collection of thirty poems written between 1892 and 1912—appeared in Britain. The following year *North of Boston*, which included his epic work "The Death of the Hired Man," was published by David Nutt. Frost, at age forty, had now earned approximately two hundred dollars from his poetry!

Near penniless when World War I broke out in 1914, he moved his family back to America. After arriving in New York City, he went to Grand Central Station on East 42nd Street and noticed a copy of a new magazine, *The New Republic*, with his name on the cover. Inside was a review, written by the American poet Amy Lowell, of his *North of Boston*, stating that the book had been published in the United States by Henry Holt and Company. Frost settled his family in the waiting room of Grand Central and walked to Holt's office on West 33rd Street. There he met Alfred Harcourt, then editor-in-chief at Holt, and learned that the wife of David Nutt had entered an agreement with Holt to publish his work in the United States—without granting any royalty to him. After the problem was cleared up, he remained with Holt throughout his entire career.

During his lifetime, honor upon honor was bestowed upon Frost; he is the only person ever to win four Pulitzer Prizes. His family life, however, was filled with personal tragedy. His sister, Jeanie, became mentally ill and was institutionalized; one daughter, Marjorie, died at birth a year after his marriage; his only son, Carol, committed suicide; another daughter, Irma, was an invalid.

In 1959, when Frost was eighty-five years old, *You Come Too*, a volume of fifty-one poems subtitled *Favorite Poems for Young Readers*, appeared. Although over the years some of his work had been used with younger readers, this book brought him further recognition among teachers, librarians, and children. Poems such as "The Pasture," "The Runaway," and "Stopping by Woods on a Snowy Evening" became widely anthologized in many textbooks used throughout the elementary and high school grades.

An invitation to participate in the inauguration of

President John F. Kennedy was a milestone in Frost's career. Television viewers across the country witnessed an unforgettable incident on that day, January 20, 1961. The sun's glare and some gusty winds prevented the poet from reading "The Gift Outright," a poem published almost twenty years before the occasion in *A Witness Tree*. Frost put the sheet of paper into his overcoat pocket and recited the verse from memory.

On March 26, 1962, on his eighty-eighth birthday, Frost was awarded the Congressional Medal at the White House by President Kennedy. His last book, *In the Clearing*, was published that same year.

He died on January 29, 1963. Upon Frost's death President Kennedy said: "His death impoverishes us all; but he has bequeathed his nation a body of imperishable verse from which Americans will gain joy and understanding."

On October 19, 1986, he was elected to the American Poets' Corner in the Cathedral of St. John the Divine in New York City.

Middle graders can read about his life and work in *A Restless Spirit: The Story of Robert Frost* by Natalie S. Bober. The biography, first published in 1981, was reissued in 1991, lavishly illustrated with photographs.

There are many biographies written for adult readers on the life of the poet. Several excellent choices include *Frost: A Literary Life Reconsidered* by William H. Pritchard, *Robert Frost Himself* by Stanley Burnshaw, and

*Robert Frost* by Jeffrey Meyers.

In 1978 Susan Jeffers, a Caldecott Honor recipient, illustrated a picture-book version of his poem *Stopping by Woods on a Snowy Evening*. Other single-volume editions include *Birches*, illustrated by Caldecott Medalist Ed Young, and *Christmas Trees*, illustrated by Ted Rand.

In 1982 Stemmer House released *A Swinger of Birches*, thirty-eight selections from his complete works, illustrated by Peter Koeppen.

Over the years many recordings of Frost reading his work have been made. There is *Robert Frost: Poems, Life, Legacy*, available on CD-ROM from Holt; this includes *The Complete Poems*, ninety minutes of Frost himself reading, 1,500 pages of letters and biographical matter—and more—a true gift!

## FROST TITLES CITED

*Birches*. Illustrated by Ed Young. Henry Holt, 1988; also in paperback.

*Boy's Will, A*. David Nutt, 1913.

*Christmas Trees*. Illustrated by Ted Rand. Henry Holt, 1990; also in paperback.

*In the Clearing*. Holt, Rinehart, 1962.

*North of Boston*. David Nutt, 1914.

*Poetry of Robert Frost, The*. Edited by Edward Connery Lathem. Holt, Rinehart, 1969; also in paperback.

*Stopping by Woods on a Snowy Evening*. Illustrated by Susan Jeffers. Dutton, 1978.

*Swinger of Birches, A: Poems of Robert Frost for Young People*.

Illustrated by Peter Koeppen. Stemmer House, 1982; also in paperback.

*Witness Tree, A.* Henry Holt, 1942.

*You Come Too: Favorite Poems for Young Readers.* Illustrated by Thomas W. Nason. Henry Holt, 1959.

## ADDITIONAL REFERENCES

Bober, Natalie S. *A Restless Spirit: The Story of Robert Frost.* Atheneum, 1981; reissued by Henry Holt, 1991.

Burnshaw, Stanley. *Robert Frost Himself.* George Braziller, 1986.

Lathem, Edward Connery. *Interviews with Robert Frost.* Holt, 1966.

Meyers, Jeffrey. *Robert Frost.* Houghton, 1996.

Pritchard, William H. *Frost: A Literary Life Reconsidered.* Oxford University Press, 1984; also in paperback.

# NIKKI GIOVANNI

*"Poetry . . .*
*tells of*
*capturing*
*a moment . . .*
*because*
*it's*
*going*
*to*
*live."*

**B**ORN YOLANDE CORNELIA GIOVANNI JR. on June 7, 1943, in Knoxville, Tennesee, Nikki Giovanni was two months old when her family moved to Cincinnati, Ohio. At age seventeen she entered Fisk University in Nashville, Tennessee, but she was expelled at the end of the first semester due to a conflict with the dean. Four years later she returned to Fisk, graduating magna cum laude in 1967. After graduation she held a variety of jobs, including that of assistant professor of English at Rutgers University in New Jersey, and consultant and columnist for such magazines as *Encore*, *American*, and *Worldwide News*.

Her first two books of adult poetry, *Black Feeling, Black Talk* and *Black Judgement*, published in 1968 and 1969, brought her national recognition. A steady stream of titles followed, each reflecting her deep involvement in African-American culture.

A collection of autobiographical essays, *Gemini*, published in 1971, was a nominee for the National Book Award. It explored her earlier years with the fierce intensity of a poet and lover of life.

Her first book for children, *Spin a Soft Black Song*, published in 1971, sprang from her volunteer activities with the Reading Is Fundamental program. A revised edition of the volume appeared in 1985, with new illustrations and a new introduction.

Other volumes for children include *Ego-Tripping*, *Vacation Time*, and *The Sun Is So Quiet*, the last title a picture-book collection of thirteen poems, twelve previously published between 1973 and 1993, illustrated by Ashley Bryan.

A prolific talent, Giovanni has also compiled several anthologies for young-adult readers, including *Grand Mothers*, a collection of poems and short stories by such authors as Gwendolyn Brooks and Gloria Naylor, and *Shimmy Shimmy Shimmy Like My Sister Kate*, a book that describes the Harlem Renaissance (1917–1935) through poems by W. E. B. Du Bois, James Weldon Johnson, Langston Hughes, Ntozake Shange, and others.

"My basic philosophy about writing for children—

or any other group—is that the reader is both interested and intelligent," Giovanni has stated. "As a lover of children's literature, I always enjoyed a good story, whether happy or sad. I think poetry, when it is most effective, tells of capturing a moment, and I make it the best I can because it's going to live.

"When I think of poems most children read, from Robert Louis Stevenson to some of the modern poets, I think of an idea being conveyed. The image is important but the idea is the heart."

In 1996 she published for adult readers *The Selected Poems of Nikki Giovanni*, 150 poems from six earlier volumes arranged chronologically. The following year *Love Poems* appeared—a book that fast became a bestseller. Other adult titles include *Cotton Candy on a Rainy Day*, *Sacred Cows—and Other Edibles*, and *Those Who Ride the Night Winds*. In all her adult books there is a bounty of work to share with teenage readers. In my work with young people I have used poems such as "My House" from *Selected Poems* with great success.

The poet loves to travel, especially to remote places away from television and the telephone. And she loves music, which is the basis of a most unusual picture book, *The Genie in the Jar*, dedicated to the singer Nina Simone, with illustrations by Caldecott Honor winner Chris Raschka.

Recipient of a host of awards including thirteen honorary doctorate degrees and keys to many cities, she currently lives in Christianberg, Virginia, where she teaches at Virginia Polytechnic Institute and State University in Blacksburg. She is the mother of one grown son, Thomas.

On the filmstrip *Nikki Giovanni* of the First Choice: Poets and Poetry series (Pied Piper Productions), she is seen strolling the streets of New York City, showing youngsters how the colors, sounds, and rhythms of sidewalk musicians and vendors can be turned into verse. Part Two of the filmstrip features a workshop lesson in which she talks about how students can make discoveries for themselves, including sensory descriptions to create a poem about rain or a picnic. Included is a teachers' guide, brief biographical information, and nine poems reprinted from various works.

In one of her essays in *Gemini* Giovanni writes: "I think we are capable of tremendous beauty once we decide we are beautiful or of giving a lot of love once we understand love is possible, and of making the world over in that image should we choose to. I really like to think a Black, beautiful loving world is possible."

*I* think anything is possible if Giovanni sets her mind to it.

## GIOVANNI TITLES CITED

*Black Feeling, Black Talk.* Afro Arts, 1968.
*Black Judgement.* Broadside Press, 1968.
*Cotton Candy on a Rainy Day.* Morrow, 1978; also in paperback.

*Ego-Tripping and Other Poems for Young People.* Illustrated by George Ford. Lawrence Hill, 1973; reissued, 1993; also in paperback.

*Gemini: An Extended Autobiographical Statement of My First Twenty-Five Years of Being a Black Poet.* Bobbs-Merrill, 1971.

*Genie in the Jar, The.* Illustrated by Chris Raschka. Henry Holt, 1996.

*Grand Mothers: Poems, Reminiscences, and Short Stories About the Keepers of Our Tradition.* Edited by Nikki Giovanni. Holt, 1994.

*Love Poems.* Morrow, 1997.

*Sacred Cows—and Other Edibles.* Morrow, 1988.

*Selected Poems of Nikki Giovanni, The.* Morrow, 1996.

*Shimmy Shimmy Shimmy Like My Sister Kate: Looking at the Harlem Renaissance Through Poems.* Edited by Nikki Giovanni. Henry Holt, 1996.

*Spin a Soft Black Song.* Illustrated by George Martins. Hill & Wang, revised edition, 1985; also in paperback.

*Sun Is So Quiet, The.* Illustrated by Ashley Bryan. Henry Holt, 1996.

*Those Who Ride the Night Winds.* Morrow, 1993; also in paperback.

*Vacation Time: Poems for Children.* Illustrated by Marisabina Russo. Morrow, 1980.

# E L O I S E
# G R E E N F I E L D

*"Give*
*children*
*words to*
*love,*
*to grow*
*on."*

Iɴ 1997 ELOISE GREENFIELD became the eleventh poet, and the first African American, to win the National Council of Teachers of English (NCTE) Award for Excellence in Poetry for Children.

After she had created a number of picture books and several biographies for children, her first book of poetry, *Honey, I Love*, appeared in 1978. It is one of her most popular collections.

She was born on May 17, 1929, in Parmele, North Carolina, the second oldest of five children; her family moved to Washington, D.C., when she was four years old. She grew up in that city and lives there now.

Despite being raised during the days of the Great

Depression, she said, "I had a wonderful childhood. We didn't have much money, but my father always had a job; we were able to manage. Both of my parents loved the arts. We went to movies and to the Howard Theater, where great jazz musicians like Duke Ellington performed."

After attending Miner Teachers College from 1946 to 1949, she held a number of jobs from clerk typist in the United States Patent Office to supervisory patent assistant.

Greenfield began writing at the age of twenty-two.

"I wrote for four and a half years before I had my first work published," she said. "My poem 'To a Violin' was published on the editorial page of the *Hartford Times* on November 6, 1962."

From that time on writing became her life's work.

In 1988 *Nathaniel Talking* appeared, nineteen poems about Nathaniel B. Free, a spirited African-American boy who raps and rhymes about a range of subjects from family to education to what it is like to be a nine-year-old. Instructions are given to readers on how to create their own twelve-bar blues poems at the back of the volume.

About *Nathaniel* Greenfield said, "Nathaniel wouldn't let go. I had planned to write only one poem. A rap poem. Mostly for fun, an excuse to play with words. And so I began, expecting to have a brief acquaintance with a small boy who loved to rap. But by the time I had written the first few words of 'Nathaniel's Rap,' I knew that the boy was not going to let go of my life and would be with me for a long time.

"Nathaniel talked, but he didn't talk to me. My characters never do, although they are aware of my presence and allow me to stay. They trust me, trust that I will treat them with respect. They recognize my need to sit in their world and watch them. And though they don't understand this strange behavior, they accept it with good humor. 'If she don't have nothing better to do than watch us, just don't pay her no mind.' And they go on about their business.

"My hope is that children who get to meet Nathaniel will find fun and inspiration in his words. For myself, giving him birth and a means of expression has been a memorable experience. I am grateful that my child, Nathaniel, was not just passing through. He came to stay."

*Night on Neighborhood Street* reflects life on a city block and the people who inhabit it—from children playing on sidewalks to an abandoned house boarded up with wooden windows that "knows that only dust rises/to dance to the lonely beat/of silence." As well as pleasant times on Neighborhood Street, Greenfield portrays problems that plague society. For example, in the verse "The Seller," she writes about a drug pusher who carries in his pockets "packages of death."

Greenfield's work differs from book to book: *Under the Sunday Tree*, twenty poems celebrating life in the Bahamas; *Kia Tanisha* and *Kia Tanisha Drives Her Car*,

single-poem board books for the youngest reader; and
*For the Love of the Game: Michael Jordan and Me*, a powerful celebration in verse contrasting the dream of the
basketball legend to that of two children finding strength
within themselves to follow their own dreams.

*Childtimes*, coauthored with her mother, Lessie Jones
Little, reflects poignant childhood memories of three
women—grandmother, mother, and daughter—who grew
up between the 1880s and the 1950s. In this volume
Greenfield states that the book is "about family . . .
about black people struggling, not to just stay alive, but
to live, to give of their talents, whether to many or few."

She comments: "What I love about writing poetry
is that you go inside yourself and write your deepest
feelings. Writing is my work. It is work that is in har-
mony with me; it sustains me. I want, through my work,
to help sustain children—to give children words to love,
to grow on.

"I usually work at home, in an office that used to be
my dining room. It's a place I love. There is art on the
walls, and a bookcase filled with children's books by
African-American authors. I have a bulletin board that
has on it photographs of people whose work I admire—
Paul Robeson, Charles Mingus, Mahalia Jackson. My
favorite time to write is from midnight to four or five in
the morning, because it's so quiet then. If I'm going to
do that, I'll take a nap during the day."

Mother of two grown children, Steven and Monica,

she travels widely speaking to children and adults about her work, often offering the message: "You're wonderful. Believe in yourself. Believe in your words and believe in your dreams."

That is good advice for all of us.

## GREENFIELD TITLES CITED

*Childtimes: A Three-Generation Memoir.* Written with Lessie Jones Little. Illustrated by Jerry Pinkney and photographs from the author's family albums. Crowell, 1979.

*For the Love of the Game: Michael Jordan and Me.* Illustrated by Jan Spivey Gilchrist. Harper, 1997.

*Honey, I Love, and Other Love Poems.* Illustrated by Leo and Diane Dillon. Crowell, 1978; also in paperback.

*Kia Tanisha.* Illustrated by Jan Spivey Gilchrist. Harper, 1997.

*Kia Tanisha Drives Her Car.* Illustrated by Jan Spivey Gilchrist. Harper, 1997.

*Nathaniel Talking.* Illustrated by Jan Spivey Gilchrist. Black Butterfly, 1988.

*Night on Neighborhood Street.* Illustrated by Jan Spivey Gilchrist. Dial, 1991.

*Under the Sunday Tree.* Illustrated by Mr. Amos Ferguson. Harper, 1988; also in paperback.

# NIKKI GRIMES

*"Poetry*
*is*
*a*
*literature*
*of*
*brushstrokes."*

"**W**ANT TO APPEAR on an International Reading Association program in Atlanta in 1997?" I asked Nikki Grimes on the telephone.

"Wow! Why not?" she exclaimed. "I've never been asked before."

In a crowded room at the convention center moments before we were to begin our program, "A Passion for Poetry," Grimes confessed to me her nervousness at appearing before a group of several hundred people. But once she began speaking, she enveloped the audience with her eloquent passion for poetry.

Grimes, born on October 20, 1950, in New York's Harlem, had a difficult childhood. Her mother, an alcoholic, divorced her husband and sent Grimes and her older sister, Carol, to separate foster homes. From ages six through ten Grimes lived in a foster home in Ossining, New York, which actually turned into a positive experience.

"These were the best and happiest of times," she told me. "It was here in a foster home, at the age of six, where I wrote my very first poem. It was also a time when I found the library. Books became my survival tool. I devoured at least five books a week. I lived in the library. At home I was the proverbial flashlight reader! Books, more than anything, were healing."

When Grimes was ten years old, she returned to live with her mother. The stressful existence of her early years continued.

"I knew I couldn't take it anymore when I returned home from junior high school one afternoon and learned my mother had destroyed all the writing I had ever done—my stories, all my notebooks filled with *words*, even a recent award I had received was thrown away— gone. She threw out everything. I left the house at the age of sixteen to live with my sister in New York City."

The painful incident didn't stop her from writing. A year later she attended a meeting at which James Baldwin spoke honoring Malcolm X. Her goal was to meet Baldwin personally. After his talk she ran down the hall after him breathlessly crying out, "Mr. Baldwin! Mr. Baldwin! Would you look at my notebook?"

He stopped, began glancing quickly at her work, and then read it straight through. Writing his name and telephone number on her notebook, he asked her to call him. She did!

"James Baldwin became my first mentor," she said. "Over the next year and a half we became friends. He encouraged me greatly.

"Another influence to my being was my father. He was the one who nurtured me in the arts. A violinist and composer, he took me to my first everything—the ballet, museums, theater. I loved him. His death was a huge loss in my life."

After high school Grimes attended Rutgers University in New Jersey, majoring in African-American studies. During this time she gave birth to a daughter. Tragedy again struck her life when the child drowned at the age of four in a neighbor's swimming pool, just prior to Grimes' receiving a Ford Foundation grant to travel to Tanzania to study the language and culture.

She went to Tanzania and stayed there for a year.

In 1977, after her first book, *Growin'*, a novel for middle readers, was published, a friend of hers began reading her work on a radio broadcast. She also brought Grimes's writing to the attention of the illustrator Tom Feelings. Soon after, Feelings asked if she would write the text for a book based on his portraits of children. This would be his first book since he had received a Caldecott Honor for Muriel Feelings' *Jambo Means Hello*.

"I literally threw Tom out of his apartment," Grimes said. "I surrounded myself with his artwork. I lived with it day and night."

The result was her first book of poetry for children, *Something on My Mind*, poems expressing emotions of children growing up.

Grimes left the United States again to live for a period of six years in Sweden, where she continued writing and became a singer. She concentrated on gospel music, appearing at the Stockholm Concert Hall. Gospel music was an important part of her upbringing.

"I was raised as a Baptist. Church life was of utmost importance," she told me. "I couldn't trust adults. God became my best friend. I talked to Him endlessly. I knew He was there for me. He was saving me throughout my childhood."

Three of her books reflect her religious upbringing.

In a foreword to *From a Child's Heart*, thirteen prayer-poems, she writes:

> *God is never far away. . . . Like the children in this book, when I was a child, I talked to God about my hopes, my fears, my longings. . . . I still do. . . . He cares. . . . He understands me, even when no one else does. I needed to know that when I was growing up. I think all children do, whether five years old or fifty.*

*Come Sunday* contains fourteen poems about LaTasha, a young girl who takes readers through various types of church worship at the Paradise Baptist Church.

"I wrote *Come Sunday* because I was tired of hearing about the negativism of church, particularly those associated with African Americans. I wanted to write something positive about a child going every Sunday to a place of comfort," she said.

*Portrait of Mary*, an exquisite fictionalized account of the life and times of the Blessed Virgin, published as an adult book, can be savored by young-adult readers.

"As a mother who has lost a child, I understand Mary's pain," she said to me. "As a Christian I understand Mary's God, and am familiar with the light that she saw at the end of the tunnel, because I have seen it too."

In 1994 *Meet Danitra Brown* was published. The endearing character, "the most splendiforous girl in town," and her best friend, Zuri Jackson, take readers on an emotional journey as the two girls face the problems and pleasures of growing up. A companion volume, *Danitra Brown Leaves Town*, is a collection of letter-poems exchanged between the two girls. Both volumes feature the energetic illustrations of Floyd Cooper.

*C Is for City*, an alphabetic picture-book rhyme, shows the vibrance of city life, from "kosher shops selling knishes" to "trains filled with tourists." Lively illustrations by Pat Cummings offer children the opportunity to search the artwork to find a host of alphabetical objects.

*It's Raining Laughter*, poems about growing up, was

inspired by the photography of Myles C. Pinkney. As with Feelings' portraits for *Something on My Mind*, she immersed herself in Pinkney's photographs to complete the text. *It's Raining Laughter* became Pinkney's first book, adding to the creative output in the field of children's literature of the talented Pinkney family.

Currently Grimes lives in Seattle, Washington. Her writing life is full. Ideas never cease.

"Define poetry for me," I asked.

She answered: "For me, poetry is a literature of brushstrokes. The poet uses a few choice words, placed just so, to paint a picture, evoke an emotion, or capture a moment in time, often though not always with the measured use of rhyme."

The last words in *It's Raining Laughter* read: "I am/joy."

Grimes is just that—*joy*—in its deepest form.

## GRIMES TITLES CITED

*C Is for City.* Illustrated by Pat Cummings. Lothrop, 1995.

*Come Sunday.* Illustrated by Michael Bryant. Eerdmans, 1996; also in paperback.

*Danitra Brown Leaves Town.* Illustrated by Floyd Cooper. Lothrop, 1998.

*From a Child's Heart.* Illustrated by Brenda Joysmith. Just Us Books, 1993.

*Growin'.* Illustrated by Charles Lilly. Dial, 1977; also in paperback.

*It's Raining Laughter.* Photographs by Myles C. Pinkney.
  Dial, 1997.
*Meet Danitra Brown.* Illustrated by Floyd Cooper. Lothrop,
  1994; also in paperback.
*Portrait of Mary.* Harcourt, 1994; also in paperback.
*Something on My Mind.* Illustrated by Tom Feelings. Dial,
  1978.

## ADDITIONAL REFERENCE

Feelings, Muriel. *Jambo Means Hello: A Swahili Alphabet
  Book.* Illustrated by Tom Feelings. Dial, 1974.

# LANGSTON HUGHES

*"Hold
fast
to
dreams . . ."*

EW POETS who have written for adults or children remain as beloved as Langston Hughes. In 1921 his first poem, "The Negro Speaks of Rivers," was published in *The Crisis* magazine, a journal edited by W. E. B. Du Bois that spoke for a recently founded organization, the National Association for the Advancement of Colored People (NAACP). Ever since, decade after decade, his multifaceted writings are read with pleasure—his writing for children as well as his work for adults: novels, short stories, autobiographies, plays, operas, operettas, newspaper columns, and a vast body of poetry.

James Mercer Langston Hughes was born on February 1, 1902, in Joplin, Missouri. His father, James Hughes, studied law, but because of the prejudice of the time he was refused the right to take his bar examination. Angry and frustrated with Jim Crow society, James

Hughes left the United States for Mexico, leaving his wife and son. Due to his mother's not being able to support both herself and young Langston, his childhood was spent shifting from one place to another, from relative to relative. Finally he went to live with his grandmother in Lawrence, Kansas. Upon his grandmother's death when he was twelve years old, he was reunited with his mother, settling in Ohio.

He attended Central High School in Cleveland, Ohio, where an English teacher, Ethel Weimer, introduced him to the work of poets, among them Walt Whitman and Carl Sandburg. In his senior year he was elected editor of the yearbook and class poet for his contributions of poems to the school newspaper.

Upon graduation Hughes went to visit his father. On a train heading south for Mexico, he wrote "The Negro Speaks of Rivers" on the back of an envelope—a verse that would become one of his best known. The month following the publication of "The Negro Speaks of Rivers" in *The Crisis*, "Aunt Sue's Stories" was also published in that journal. He soon became known as the the Black Poet Laureate, and from that time on his work frequently appeared in *The Crisis*.

He began a series of wanderings across the world—to Europe, Russia, and Africa. While traveling, he worked at a variety of jobs, from dishwashing in a Parisian café to ranching in Mexico.

Hughes' first book of poetry, *The Weary Blues*, was

published for adults in 1926. From this time on he appeared in print regularly.

Hughes completed his college education in 1929, graduating from Lincoln University in Pennsylvania, a college for African-American men. After a great deal of continous world travel, he moved to Harlem, in New York City, where he lived until his death on May 22, 1967.

In 1971 the artist Romare Bearden created a six-panel collage that he called *The Block*, now in the collection of the Metropolitan Museum of Art in New York City, which pays tribute to neighborhood life in Harlem. Lowery S. Sims and Daisy Murray Voight chose thirteen of Hughes' poems to match selections of Bearden's vibrant, full-color pieces and published the creative collaboration in a volume entitled *The Block*. The pairing is particularly interesting because Bearden and Hughes knew one another in Harlem in the late 1930s, when Bearden established his first studio on 125th Street. An introduction to the book is written by Bill Cosby.

Interest in Hughes continues strong in the 1990s with the reissue of *Popo and Fifina*, a novel for young readers that Hughes coauthored with Arna Bontemps, and the appearance of a never-before-published tale, *The Pasteboard Bandit*, also coauthored with Bontemps. *The Collected Poems of Langston Hughes*, edited by Arnold Rampersad, has also been published.

*The Dream Keeper*, published for children in 1932,

when he was thirty years old, contains some of the finest twentieth-century poetry ever written; the book was reissued in 1994, with seven additional poems and black-and-white woodcut engravings by Caldecott Honor recipient Brian Pinkney.

Having admired Hughes' work throughout my life, and having edited a collection of his poetry, *Don't You Turn Back*, I had the great honor of being asked to do the introduction to the 1994 edition of *The Dream Keeper*. In it I wrote:

> *Little did he know that more than six decades after* The Dream Keeper and Other Poems *first appeared . . . his passionate, sensitive, strong, and mighty words would continue to be sung, shouted, whispered, hummed—from farmlands to suburbs, from cities to countrysides all over the world.*
>
> *Hopes, dreams, aspirations, life, and love are embodied in his poetry—poems about his people, for his people, poems for each and every one of us, universalities that humankind of all ages and races have struggled for and will continue to strive for as long as we are on this earth.*

A not-to-be-missed reissue of the cassette *The Dream Keeper and Other Poems* has been released by Smithsonian Folkways. Students can hear from the master himself how his poetry developed from specific experiences and ideas. Warm and witty, he talks about how a trip to the waterfront inspired "Water-Front Streets"; how a beloved woman's memory of slavery sparked "Aunt Sue's Stories"; how his belief that people—all people—should treasure their dreams inspired his famous poem "Dreams." The narrative leads naturally into each of his selections; the script is biographical.

Over the years many biographies have been written about the life and times of Hughes. Several of them are by prominent personalities who knew and worked with him.

Although *Black Troubador: Langston Hughes* by Charlemae Hill Rollins is out of print, it is well worth seeking in library collections. Rollins, a renowned children's librarian who met Hughes when he was a young man, includes in her volume many rare black-and-white photographs and letter facsimiles.

Milton Meltzer, a friend of Hughes' who collaborated with him on two adult books, wrote the biography *Langston Hughes* shortly after the poet's death. It is a volume to put at the top of your list. A runner-up for a 1969 National Book Award, the biography was reissued in 1997, in a new large format with illustrations by Stephen Alcorn.

Ossie Davis, the distinguished actor-playwright, was influenced by Hughes' poems when he first encountered them as a high-school student in Waycross, Georgia. He and his wife, actress Ruby Dee, became friends of Hughes' in the years after World War II, when the poet lived in Harlem. Davis' *Langston: A Play* is set in the early 1900s, with a cast of nine characters. Excerpts from Hughes' poems are interwoven with the dialogue.

Two other biographies include *Coming Home: From the Life of Langston Hughes*, a picture book by Floyd Cooper focusing on Hughes' childhood years, and *Free to Dream* by Audrey Osofsky, containing a host of vintage black-and-white photographs and a musical composition she wrote based on Hughes' poem "Dreams."

Adult references include *Arna Bontemps–Langston Hughes Letters, 1925–1927*, selected and edited by Charles H. Nichols; *Langston Hughes: Before and Beyond Harlem* by Faith Berry; and *The Life of Langston Hughes: Volume 1, 1902–1944: I, Too, Sing America* and *Volume 2: I Dream a World*, by Arnold Rampersad.

The cassette *The Voice of Langston Hughes*, for mature listeners, also released by Smithsonian Folkways, features the poet talking about the creation of twenty-one verses, including "The Negro Speaks of Rivers," "Mother to Son," and several prayers he penned.

Ironically, despite his extraordinary literary output, Hughes lived in poverty most of his life. He said to Arna Bontemps, "Fame is lovely—but hard to eat."

Many eulogies have been written about the poet and his contributions to American literature. Perhaps the most tender was one created by a fourth-grade student in Harlem whom I worked with. She wrote this poem the day after Hughes died:

In Memoriam to Langston Hughes
The Useless Pen

*A pen lay useless on his desk.*
*A mother once held a babe on her breast.*
*Where is the lad this very day?*
*Down by Poetry Bay they say,*
*Where the Poets sit and think all day*
*Of a way to make people happy.*
*Even though they are not here today*
*I know they meet by Poetry Bay*
*Trying to think of a special way*
*To welcome Langston to Poetry Bay.*

## HUGHES TITLES CITED

*The Block: Poems.* Edited by Lowery S. Sims and Daisy Murray Voight. Illustrated by Romare Bearden. Viking, 1995.

*Collected Poems of Langston Hughes, The.* Edited by Arnold Rampersad and David Roessel. Knopf, 1994.

*Don't You Turn Back: Poems.* Selected by Lee Bennett Hopkins. Illustrated by Ann Grifalconi. Knopf, 1969.

*Dream Keeper and Other Poems, The.* Illustrated by Helen Sewall. Knopf, 1932; reissued 1994 with illustrations by Brian Pinkney; also in paperback.

*Pasteboard Bandit, The.* Written with Arna Bontemps. Illustrated by Peggy Turley. Oxford, 1997.

*Popo and Fifina: Children of Haiti.* Illustrated by E. Simms Campbell. Macmillan, 1932; reissued by Oxford University Press, 1993.

*Weary Blues, The.* Knopf, 1926.

## ADDITIONAL REFERENCES

Berry, Faith. *Langston Hughes, Before and Beyond Harlem.* Lawrence Hill, 1983; also in paperback.

Cooper. Floyd, *Coming Home: From the Life of Langston Hughes.* Philomel, 1994; also in paperback.

Davis, Ossie. *Langston: A Play.* Delacorte, 1982.

Meltzer, Milton. *Langston Hughes: A Biography.* Crowell, 1968; reissued with illustrations by Stephen Alcorn, Millbrook Press, 1997; also in paperback.

Nichols, Charles H., editor. *Arna Bontemps–Langston Hughes Letters, 1925–1967.* Dodd, Mead, 1980.

Osofsky, Audrey. *Free to Dream: The Making of a Poet: Langston Hughes.* Lothrop, 1996.

Rampersad, Arnold. *The Life of Langston Hughes: Volume 1, 1902–1941: I, Too, Sing America.* Oxford University Press, 1986; *Volume 2: I Dream a World.* Oxford University Press, 1988; both volumes also in paperback.

Rollins, Charlemae Hill. *Black Troubador: Langston Hughes.* Rand McNally, 1970.

# X. J. KENNEDY

*"Poetry
helps us
travel
beyond
ourselves."*

**X**. J. KENNEDY was born on August 21, 1929, in Dover, New Jersey, where he was raised. His mother was a trained nurse, and his father was a timekeeper in a boiler factory.

Preoccupied with writing from the age of nine or ten, Kennedy published homemade comic books and peddled them for nickels to friends. He also became the editor-in-chief of a women's magazine with a circulation of one—his mother!

"After college," he states, "I determined on a career as a writer for science fiction magazines, but at the end of six months had sold only two fifty-dollar stories, and so ignobly abandoned the field to Isaac Asimov. After a hitch in the Navy, then a year in Paris studying French irregular verbs on the G.I. Bill, I stumbled into college teaching and eventually became an English professor at Tufts University, near Boston, Massachusetts. In 1977 I left teaching to write for a living, and have been doing so happily ever since."

His first book, *Nude Descending a Staircase*, a collection of poems for adults, appeared in 1961, followed by two more collections and a volume of selected poems, published in England.

Until 1975 he was best known as a writer for adults. He also wrote, and continues to write, fiction, nonfiction, and textbooks, including *An Introduction to Poetry*, which has been used by more than a million college students.

For years he wrote poetry for children but did not try to have it published. One day, in the 1970s, he received a letter from Myra Cohn Livingston, who had enjoyed *Nude Descending a Staircase*, and wanted to know if he had written verse for children. Via Livingston, Margaret K. McElderry, the renowned editor, heard about Kennedy and invited him to send his writing for children to her. The result was *One Winter Night in August*, published in 1975. Since that date he has continued to publish books of verse with McElderry, including *The Phantom Ice Cream Man*; *The Forgetful Wishing Well*; *Ghastlies, Goops & Pincushions*; *The Kite That Braved Old Orchard Beach*; *Uncle Switch*; and a trilogy featuring irreverent children—*Brats*, *Drat These Brats*, and *Fresh Brats*.

In 1992 Kennedy departed from much of the light

verse he had previously penned, creating *The Beasts of Bethlehem*, nineteen poems told from the point of view of creatures present at the Nativity and what they might have said on that night of nights.

The book garnered rave reviews, including one in the *Bulletin of the Center for Children's Books* in which Betsy Hearne, then editor, stated that he "has crowned his rich career."

Ideas for his work start with small fragments of language.

"I begin with a couple of lines that rhyme or just a few words, and if they look like a poem I go on with them," Kennedy writes. "Not all of these fragments develop into poems. I have several packing cases full of fragments that have gone no place. After a while I look at them again in case they're ready to go someplace. I have never been able to write what is termed free verse. I love the constant surprise one encounters in rhyming things, and the driving urge of the steady beat."

Pleased with the trend of increased use of literature in textbooks, he says: "This movement has opened up poetry to younger and younger listeners. I'm keenly interested in this development and hope soon to supply more new verse for these little squirts—if they will stand for it.

"Poetry makes kids more aware of language and wakes them up to the real world. Kids spend so much time watching television; poetry reminds them that they have senses besides sight, and that the world is full of wonderful things."

For many years he has lived in Bedford, Massachusetts, with his wife, Dorothy, who has collaborated with her husband on *Knock at a Star: A Child's Introduction to Poetry* and *Talking Like the Rain*, a compilation of more than one hundred poems with full-color illustrations by Jane Dyer.

"Our girl and four boys," says Kennedy, "born between 1963 and 1972, have been friendly but supportive critics; and while I've subtly urged them to love poetry—anybody's—I have to admit that poetry is a little farther down their ladder of love objects than sports, ice skating, electronic rock music, movies, or videotapes. But such is life."

The *X* in his name was chosen arbitrarily "to distinguish me from the better-known Kennedys."

## KENNEDY TITLES CITED

*Beasts of Bethlehem, The: Verse.* Illustrated by Michael McCurdy. McElderry, 1992.

*Brats.* Illustrated by James Watt. Atheneum, 1986; also in paperback.

*Drat These Brats!* Illustrated by James Watts. McElderry, 1993.

*Forgetful Wishing Well, The.* Illustrated by Monica Incisa. Atheneum, 1985.

*Fresh Brats.* Illustrated by James Watts. McElderry, 1990.

*Ghastlies, Goops & Pincushions*. Illustrated by Ron Barrett. McElderry, 1989.

*Introduction to Poetry, An*, 4th edition. Little, Brown, 1978.

*Kite That Braved Old Orchard Beach, The: Year-Round Poems for Young People*. Illustrated by Marian Young. McElderry, 1991.

*Knock at a Star: A Child's Introduction to Poetry*. Edited by X. J. Kennedy and Dorothy M. Kennedy. Illustrated by Karen Ann Weinhaus. Little, Brown, 1982; also in paperback.

*Nude Descending a Staircase*. Doubleday, 1961; 2nd edition, Carnegie Mellon, 1995.

*One Winter Night in August, and Other Nonsense Jingles*. Illustrated by David McPhail. Atheneum, 1975.

*Phantom Ice Cream Man, The: More Nonsense Verse*. Illustrated by David McPhail, Atheneum, 1979.

*Talking Like the Rain: A First Book of Poems*. Compiled by X. J. Kennedy and Dorothy M. Kennedy. Illustrated by Jane Dyer. Little, Brown, 1992.

*Uncle Switch: Loony Limericks*. Illustrated by John O'Brien. McElderry, 1997.

# KARLA KUSKIN

*"Poetry
can be
as natural
and effective
a form of
self-expression
as
singing
and
shouting. "*

KARLA KUSKIN, a native New Yorker, was born on July 7, 1932. She attended the Little Red School House in the heart of Greenwich Village. From her earliest childhood years poetry has had a special place in her life.

"As a young child I would make up rhymes, which my mother wrote down and read back to me. My father wrote verse to and *for* me. As I began to learn to read, I was encouraged by my parents to read aloud. I was also fortunate that at the Little Red School House I had teachers who read poetry aloud, who greatly influenced my love of verse. Poetry was food and drink!"

She recalls her mother giving her *Old Possum's Book of Practical Cats* by T. S. Eliot when she was seven years old, "a gift that was the most wondrous thing I could imagine." She adds, "I guess I grew up with a metronomic beat inside my head, which fortunately never left."

Kuskin's first book, *Roar and More*, published in 1956, began as a project for a graphic arts class at the Yale School of Design, where she graduated in 1955 with a B.F.A. degree. The book was reissued in 1990 in a vibrant, full-color new edition. Many volumes of verse followed *Roar and More*, including *Near the Window Tree*, a collection of poetry containing notes to readers about the development of her writings.

"*Near the Window Tree* is my most personal book of verse," she states. "Not only are the notes helpful to teachers, they give a lot of insight to readers."

*Dogs & Dragons, Trees & Dreams* contains many of her best-loved works written between 1958 and 1975, illustrated with her lively black-and-white drawings. Through introductions and notes about her poems, she leads readers on an enchanting tour of the world of poetry, telling how and why some of the poems "happened," how rhythm, rhyme, and word sounds continue to "stick in the mind and stay on the tongue for a lifetime."

One of these notes reads:

*If there were a recipe for a poem, there would be ingredients: word sounds, rhythm, description, feeling, memory, rhyme, and imagination. They can be put together a thousand different ways, a thousand, thousand . . . more. If you and I were to go at the same time to the same party for the same person, our descriptions would be different. As different as we are from each other. It is those differences that make our poems interesting.*

Some of the delights in this volume include "Lewis Had a Trumpet," about a boy who is too fond of the instrument, and "Catherine," about a girl who bakes a most delicious mud, weeds, and gravel cake. "I Woke Up This Morning," perfect for reading aloud, or even yelling aloud, is three pages long, telling of a child who wakes up and can do nothing right all day; as the child's frustrations mount, so does the size of the type on the pages, becoming larger and larger, as the poem becomes funnier and funnier.

Another Kuskin volume is *The Sky Is Always in the Sky,* a collection of thirty-five previously published verses along with one new piece she penned especially for the book.

One of Kuskin's concerns regarding poetry centers on the tendency to overanalyze and dissect her work as well as the work of others. She expressed her philosophy in this poignant letter she sent to me:

*If I were to introduce you to someone I care for*
*I might say*

*"This is my friend Sue*
*I like her very much and therefore*
*I hope you will like her too."*
*However*
*after your meeting with Sue*
*I would not ask you to explain*
*her psychological and chemical makeup*
*or the genetic reason her eyes are $\frac{1}{3}$ grey*
*and $\frac{2}{3}$rds blue,*
*nor would I demand an interminable essay*
*on Sue's ethnicity*
*education*
*blood pressure*
*taste in furniture*
*or home.*
*And*
*that's the way I feel about poetry.*
*If I want to introduce a poem to you,*
*I will simply open up a book and say*
*"I would like you to meet a friend of mine.*
*My friend happens to be a poem."*

*(And you leave your dissecting tools at home.)*

Kuskin has written several highly acclaimed picture books in prose, including *The Philharmonic Gets Dressed*, joyously describing how 105 members of an orchestra prepare for an eight-thirty P.M. performance. The book grew from her children's interest in watching their father, an oboe player, getting dressed one evening for a concert.

In addition to her many other accomplishments, she designed the official medallion for the National Council of Teachers of English (NCTE) Award for Excellence in Poetry for Children and received the award herself in 1979.

Kuskin has written: "The French critic Joseph Joubert once said, 'You will find poetry nowhere unless you bring some of it with you.' To which might be added that if you do bring some of it with you, you will find it everywhere."

She can be seen on the filmstrip *Karla Kuskin* in the First Choice: Poets and Poetry series (Pied Piper Productions). Part Two of the strip features a workshop lesson giving students the opportunity to be anything they might like to be—a chair or a strawberry, a curious mouse or a baseball with a headache—and to create rhymed or unrhymed verses about these objects. A teachers' guide, photograph, brief biographical information, and ten poems reprinted from her various books are part of the set.

A more recent interview appears on the video-cassette "Good Conversations: Karla Kuskin" (Tim Podell Productions), set in her Brooklyn Heights home.

In 1995 Kuskin's delightful picture-book autobiography, *Thoughts, Pictures, and Words*, was published, featuring full-color photographs by her son, Nicholas.

## KUSKIN TITLES CITED

*Dogs & Dragons, Trees & Dreams.* Harper, 1980; also in paperback.

*Near the Window Tree.* Harper, 1975.

*Philharmonic Gets Dressed, The.* Illustrated by Marc Simont. Harper, 1982; also in paperback.

*Roar and More.* Harper, 1956; reissued with new illustrations, 1990; also in paperback.

*Sky Is Always in the Sky, The.* Illustrated by Isabelle Dervaux. Harper, 1998.

*Thoughts, Pictures, and Words.* Illustrated by Nicholas Kuskin. Owens, 1995.

## ADDITIONAL REFERENCE

*Eliot, T. S. Old Possum's Book of Practical Cats.* Illustrated by Edward Gorey. New edition, Harcourt, 1982; also in paperback.

# J.   PATRICK   LEWIS

*"Poetry is*

*a*

*blind date*

*with*

*enchantment."*

"**I** LOVE TO EXPERIMENT with language, with a variety of meters, forms, rhyme schemes. I'm always on the lookout for the new," says J. Patrick Lewis.

In 1990 Lewis burst into the poetic world with *A Hippopotamusn't*, thirty-five witty animal verses. *Booklist* heralded his debut stating, "If wordplay were an Olympic event, Lewis could go for the gold."

During the 1990s he created both light and serious verse in numerous books, such as *Two-Legged, Four-Legged, No-Legged Rhymes* and *Ridicholas Nicholas*, two more books of animal poems, as well as *July Is a Mad Mosquito*, a tribute to each month of the year, and *Earth Verses and Water Rhymes*, which celebrates nature. Lewis has also written picture-book narrative verse stories such as *The Boat of Many Rooms: The Story of Noah in Verse* and *The La-di-da Hare*, a rollicking tale that *Publishers Weekly* described as a "spirited romp" that "echoes classical nonsense poetry."

In *Black Swan/White Crow* he creates haiku via thirteen selections in a spare, elegant edition illustrated with color woodcuts by Chris Manson.

Born on May 5, 1942, in Gary, Indiana, Lewis told me he had a "disgustingly normal happy childhood" growing up with two brothers—one a twin.

Lewis, who holds a Ph.D. in economics, knew early in life that he wanted to become a college teacher, a goal he reached at the age of twenty-five. Currently he teaches economics at Otterbein College in Westerville, Ohio, where he lives.

"I teach such subjects as microtheory, comparative economic systems, and Third World economics and developments," he said, "while I continue to write children's books."

His interest in writing for children began with a trip he took with his wife and children to Cumberland Falls, Kentucky, to see a moonbow, a natural phenomenon occurring only two places in the world—there and in Africa. The book about the experience, *The Moonbow of Mr. B. Jones*, a delightful mountain tale written in the 1970s, wasn't published until 1992.

"My 'first' book actually was my *fifth* book to be published," he said.

It was poetry, however, that had become a passion.

"In 1983," he said, "I sent some poems to Myra Cohn Livingston. Two weeks later she called me from her home in Beverly Hills, to ask if I had written any Christmas poems. I hadn't. Myra asked if I would write some. I still remember shaking on the telephone as I talked to her. I wrote several poems and sent them to her. She used two of my limericks in her collection *Christmas Poems*. These became my first published verse."

Soon after the publication of *Christmas Poems*, Livingston told me of "this incredible young talent whose words were spun of magic," and suggested that I get in touch with him. I did. Since that time Lewis and I have met, exchanged numerous letters, and talked and talked on the telephone. His work appears in many of my anthologies.

Totally dedicated to the craft of writing, he does an extensive amount of research on any subject he writes about, whether it is a robin playing "tug-of-worm" or a red fox "yipping when the moon is down." He rewrites and rewrites in constant search for a perfect word or phrase.

"Poetry is as much rewriting as it is writing," Lewis explained. "Every word must be absolutely right. In many cases what readers see on a printed page is the fifth, tenth, or twenty-fifth revision of a poem."

He juggles many projects at the same time, moving from manuscript to manuscript—prose to poetry—teaching in the mornings, writing in the afternoons. Recently he decided, after a great deal of thought, to visit schools.

"For years I avoided classroom visits," he told me. "The reason was pure unadulterated *fear*! I was convinced that a school visit with me would produce utter mayhem. I knew I had 'control' over my captive audiences of college students—but with children I kept thinking, 'What would I do with them?' I quickly learned how wrong I was. It has become a thrilling experience to share my work with young children. The more I visit schools, and I'm doing it a lot lately, the more I'm learning to do more of a performance. I'm becoming a ham!"

Lewis travels a great deal and has a particular passion for Russia.

"In 1972, while working on my dissertation, I was chosen as an International Research and Exchange Fellow. As part of the program my family and I went to live in Moscow for a year while I finished my dissertation. The entire experience was both fascinating and difficult. I return to the country often. Some of my dearest friends in the world live there," he says.

His love of that country is reflected in several picture books, including *The Tsar and the Amazing Cow*, an original folk tale, and *The Frog Princess*, a retelling of the Russian legend, illustrated by Gennady Spirin.

Lewis is the father of three grown children, Beth, Matt, and Leigh Ann, "my biggest fans and biggest critics!"

"What is poetry?" I asked him.

With little hesitation he replied, "Poetry is a blind

date with enchantment." He quickly asked, "Is that okay, Lee?"

I thought it was wonderfully "okay."

Readers of all ages can revel in his multifaceted writings—what a blind date they have in store for them!

## LEWIS TITLES CITED

*Black Swan/White Crow: Haiku*. Illustrated by Chris Manson. Atheneum, 1995.

*Boat of Many Rooms, The: The Story of Noah in Verse*. Illustrated by Reg Cartwright. Atheneum, 1997.

*Earth Verses and Water Rhymes*. Illustrated by Robert Sabuda. Atheneum, 1991.

*Frog Princess, The:* A Russian Folktale. Illustrated by Gennady Spirin. Dial, 1994.

*Hippopotamusn't and Other Animal Poems, A*. Illustrated by Victoria Chess. Dial, 1990; also in paperback.

*July Is a Mad Mosquito*. Illustrated by Melanie W. Hall. Atheneum, 1994.

*La-di-da Hare, The*. Illustrated by Diane Cain Blusenthal. Atheneum, 1997.

*Moonbow of Mr. B. Jones, The*. Illustrated by Dirk Zimmer. Knopf, 1992.

*Riddle-icious*. Illustrated by Debbie Tilley. Knopf, 1996.

*Ridicholas Nicholas: More Animal Poems*. Illustrated by Victoria Chess. Dial, 1995.

*Tsar and the Amazing Cow, The*. Illustrated by Friso Henstra. Dial, 1988.

*Two-Legged, Four-Legged, No-Legged Rhymes*. Illustrated by Pamela Paparone. Knopf, 1991.

## ADDITIONAL REFERENCE

Livingston, Myra Cohn, editor. *Christmas Poems*. Illustrated by Trina Schart Hyman. Holiday House, 1984.

# MYRA COHN LIVINGSTON

*"Poetry*
*comes in*
*strange ways*
*and never*
*at the moment*
*when one*
*might think*
*it*
*should*
*come."*

MYRA COHN LIVINGSTON was born on August 17, 1926, in Omaha, Nebraska. Her family moved to California when she was eleven years old. There she began her creative career as a musician and writer. She studied the French horn from ages twelve through twenty, becoming so accomplished that she was invited to join the Los Angeles Philharmonic Orchestra at the age of sixteen.

"I had an ideal, happy childhood. I had wise and

wonderful parents who taught me that a busy creative life brings much happiness," she said.

She began writing poetry while a freshman at Sarah Lawrence College in New York.

"I turned in some poems that my professor, Katherine Liddell, felt were for children. She urged me to submit them to *Story Parade* magazine, and in 1946 'Whispers' became my first published poem.

"I submitted a complete manuscript, *Whispers and Other Poems*, to several publishing houses; it was rejected. Margaret K. McElderry, then at Harcourt, Brace, urged me, however, to continue writing. Twelve years later I sent the manuscript—rewritten—back to Harcourt; it was accepted and published in 1958."

The relationship between Livingston and McElderry continued to the time of Livingston's death. With McElderry she created more than twenty-five volumes, including *B Is for Baby*, inspired by her first grandchild, Richard Gibbons, and the posthumously published *Cricket Never Does*, a collection of sixty-seven haiku and tanka verses.

In addition to volumes of poems, she wrote nonfiction books for both children and adults and a plethora of critical essays.

Livingston prided herself on the fact that she had true respect for the craft and form of poetry.

"Trained as a traditionalist in poetry, I feel strongly about the importance of order imposed by fixed forms, meter, and rhyme when I write about some things; yet free verse seems more suitable for other subjects. It is the force of what I say that shapes the form.

"Poetry, because it is succinct, because it humanizes, and because it carries within it the form and language of change, is of vital importance.

"Poetry comes in strange ways and never at the moment when one might think it should come. There are poems I have tried to write for twenty years that have never come out right. Others seem to come in a flash. Searching for the right form to express certain ideas takes time," she commented to me.

*Sky Songs*, for example, consists of fourteen works about the varied aspects of the sky, such as the moon, planets, shooting stars, and smog. Each poem is constructed in a fifteen-line, three-stanza cinquain form—the only work of its kind available to date.

*Up in the Air*, a picture book describing the sensation of flying in an airplane, is created entirely in triplets.

*Festivals*, which describes through fourteen poems celebrations observed throughout the world—from Chinese New Year and Tet Nguyen-Dan to Mardi Gras and Kwanzaa—features a wide mastery of verse forms. In it are to be found cinquain series, free verse, haiku, and even a playlet, "Las Posadas: (The Inns)," a two-page rhyme written entirely in couplets.

Regarding her work habits, Livingston once said, "Writing is no easy task; it is very difficult work. Nothing that comes easily is worth as much as that which is worked at, which develops through the important process of growing, discarding, and keeping only the best."

During her lifetime she received numerous awards for her extraordinary accomplishments, including the 1980 National Council of Teachers of English (NCTE) Award for Excellence in Poetry for Children.

Livingston edited outstanding anthologies for young-adult readers. Her first collection, *A Tune Beyond Us*, published in 1968, contains a wealth of work by world voices. Represented are American writers such as David McCord, May Swenson, and Walt Whitman; English writers Walter de la Mare, Edward Lear, Gerard Manley Hopkins; Spanish works by Federico García Lorca and Juan Ramón Jiménez; Russian voices of Andrei Voznesensky and Yevgeny Yevtushenko.

Not content with translations, she chose to have many of the compositions printed in their *original* languages, so those who read other languages could enjoy the music of the originals.

In a fitting Editor's Note to the book she wrote: "In an age of science and definition, it sometimes seems important to reflect that art escapes definition by its appeal to man's senses, sensitivities, and emotions. Poetry is a place where we are not expected to define or analyze or answer questions. We can simply laugh or cry or wonder—or turn the page until we find a poem that sings the tune we wish to hear. It's as easy as that."

Although *A Tune Beyond Us* is out of print, it is worth looking for in library collections.

Sharing her expertise was an immensely important part of Livingston's life. Beginning in 1973 she taught a Master Class in Poetry at the University of California in Los Angeles. The result of her teaching appears in the posthumously published *I Am Writing a Poem About . . . A Game of Poetry*, based on an assignment she gave to use a specific word or words in an original poem, such as "rabbit," or "ring, drum, blanket." The volume features work by such exceptional new poetic voices in the field of children's literature as Tony Johnston, Alice Schertle, Monica Gunning, Janet S. Wong, Joan Bransfield Graham, and Deborah Chandra.

In 1991, to further share her expertise, she wrote *Poem-Making: Ways to Begin Writing Poetry*, a handbook that introduces readers—and future writers—to the different voices of poetry. Not only is this a unique guide for young writers to use for creating their own poems, it is a book I recommend to any adult who wishes to explore the genre.

"*Poem-Making* is the result of about thirty years of teaching in the Dallas Public Library and the Dallas and Beverly Hills schools (kindergarten through high school for eighteen years), and conducting poetry workshops throughout the country both as a teacher and poet," she said.

"I think I was spurred on to write it because of the constant contact with children. I wrote two adult books on the subject of children writing poetry, *When You Are Alone/It Keeps You Capone* and *The Child as Poet*. I felt that children are given so much misinformation about poetry writing from such a variety of sources, I wanted to pass on the craft I had learned from poets such as Robert Fitzgerald and Horace Gregory, with whom I studied in college. One notices, for example, that few people teach metrics anymore, so children have no way of getting this information.

"To my knowledge *Poem-Making* is the first book for children on the subject of poetry that is written by someone who is both a children's poet and teacher."

A sixteen-page personal essay on her life and career, filled with black-and-white photographs, appears in *Something About the Author: Autobiographical Series*, edited by Adele Sarkissian. In this fact-filled account you will find marvelous anecdotes about her meeting and marrying Richard R. Livingston; the birth of her three children, Josh, Jonas, and Jennie; her incredible stints as secretary to the singer-actress Dinah Shore and the violinist Jascha Heifetz; and more of her sage philosophy.

In the filmstrip *Myra Cohn Livingston* in the First Choice: Poets and Poetry series (Pied Piper Productions) she discusses her work, making viewers aware of their own varied feelings and how they can be used as a starting point for writing. In Part Two of the filmstrip a workshop lesson helps young writers use the couplet form to create a poem based on feelings, such as disappointment. Included are a teachers' guide, a photograph, brief biographical information, and eight poems reprinted from her various books published between 1958 and 1976.

Another way to bring Livingston's work into the classroom is via *Celebrations*, a kit available from Wonderstorms/World Almanac Education. The package includes ten extraordinary posters featuring full-color paintings by Leonard Everett Fisher and Livingston's poems from *Celebrations*, a collection of sixteen poems on holidays, including "Martin Luther King Day," "Presidents' Day," and "Passover."

On August 23, 1996, Livingston died at her home in Beverly Hills, California. I miss her elegance, her eloquence, her charm, her wit, our "friendly-fire" arguments that went on and on into the wee hours of the morning.

But her work continues. Her voice will be heard by generations of children to come.

Livingston's whispers, soft as skin, tickled our ears. How LOUD her whispers were—are—will *be*.


## LIVINGSTON TITLES CITED

*B Is for Baby: An Alphabet of Verses.* Illustrated by Steel
  Stillman. McElderry, 1996.
*Celebrations.* Illustrated by Leonard Everett Fisher. Holiday
  House, 1985; also in paperback.

*Cricket Never Does: A Collection of Haiku and Tanka.*
Illustrated by Kees de Krefte. McElderry, 1997.

*Festivals.* Illustrated by Leonard Everett Fisher. Holiday
House, 1996.

*I Am Writing A Poem About . . . A Game of Poetry.*
McElderry, 1997.

*Poem-Making: Ways to Begin Writing Poetry.* Harper, 1991.

*Sky Songs.* Illustrated by Leonard Everett Fisher. Holiday
House, 1984.

*Tune Beyond Us, A: A Collection of Poetry.* Compiled by
Myra Cohn Livingston. Harcourt, 1968.

*Up in the Air.* Illustrated by Leonard Everett Fisher. Holiday
House, 1989.

*When You Are Alone/It Keeps You Capone: An Approach to
Creative Writing for Children.* Atheneum, 1973.

*Whispers and Other Poems.* Illustrated by Jacqueline Chwast.
Harcourt, 1958.

# DAVID McCORD

*"Poetry*
*is so*
*many things*
*besides*
*the*
*shiver*
*down*
*the*
*spine."*

WHEN DAVID McCORD died on April 13, 1997, at the age of ninety-nine, in Boston, Massachusetts, the *New York Times* obituary described him as "Prolific Poet Who Won the Hearts of Children." And indeed he did! And does! And will!

McCord's poetic subjects range from varied aspects of nature to a trip to a Laundromat. He wrote for both children and adults; in an interview he commented to me on this duality:

"Poetry for children is simpler than poetry for adults. The overtones are fewer, but it should have overtones.

Basically, of course, it isn't different. Children's verse sometimes turns out, or is turned out, to be not much more than doggerel—lame lines, limp rhymes, poor ideas. By and large, verse written for children is rhymed; it is nearly always brief, though an occasional poem in the hands of a skilled performer like Ogden Nash, who was a dear friend of mine, may tell a story."

Over the course of many years I had long conversations with McCord. At times he talked as if *he* were a living poem. Throughout my career I have read and heard hundreds of definitions of what poetry is, what poetry should be. No one has ever put the genre in its proper place as he did.

In my book *Pauses* I include a quote from him— one of the most exquisite statements I ever heard regarding poetry—one that I wish would reach out to every reader, everywhere.

When I asked him, "What is poetry? What is poetry to *you?*" he replied:

*Poetry, like rain, should fall with elemental music, and poetry for children should catch the eye as well as the ear and the mind. It should delight, it really* has *to delight. Furthermore, poetry for children should keep reminding them, without any feeling on their part that they are being reminded, that the English language is a most marvelous and availing instrument.*

*Poetry is so many things besides the shiver down the*

*spine. It is a new day lying on a new doorstep. It is what will stir the weariest mind to write. It is the inevitable said so casually that the reader or listener thinks he said it himself. It is the fall of syllables that run as easily as water flowing over a dam. It is fireflies in May, apples in October, the wood fire burning when one looks up from an open book. It is the best dream from which one ever waked too soon. It is* Peer Gynt *and* Moby Dick *in a single line. It is the best translation of words that do not exist. It is hot coffee dripping from an icicle. It is the accident involving sudden life. It is the calculus of the imagination. It is the finishing touch to what one could not finish. It is a hundred things as unexplainable as all our foolish explanations.*

McCord's first book of poetry for children, *Far and Few, Rhymes of the Never Was and Always Is*, appeared in 1952, twenty-five years after his first book of poems for adults was published. He told me how he entered the field of children's poetry.

"Two years after I finished my master's degree in English at Harvard—I had previously studied to become a physicist—I wrote a number of poems for children. One was published in the *Saturday Review of Literature* and got into some anthologies. I seemed to know instinctively that to write for the young, I had to write for myself, out of myself, about things I did as a boy, about things that are fairly timeless as subjects. I do not believe that one can teach the art of writing. You are born with the urge for it or you are not. Only the hardest self-discipline and considerable mastery of self-criticism will get you anywhere."

In 1977 he became the first recipient of the National Council of Teachers of English (NCTE) Award for Excellence in Poetry for Children. That same year *One at a Time: His Collected Poems for the Young* was published, a 494-page volume of verse containing poems from seven earlier titles. The volume features an introduction by McCord and includes a very useful subject index. Beloved works such as "Every Time I Climb a Tree," "The Star in the Pail," and "This Is My Rock" are in this treasury. Three years later *Speak Up* appeared, and in 1990, when he was ninety-three, a poem commissioned by Myra Cohn Livingston appeared in her anthology *Poems for Grandmothers*.

McCord was born on November 15, 1897, at 9 East 10th Street, in the heart of New York's Greenwich Village. He grew up on Long Island, in Princeton, New Jersey, and in Oregon.

As a child McCord was stricken with malaria. Recurring bouts of fever kept him out of school a great deal. This, however, did not stop him from graduating with high honors from Lincoln High School in Portland, Oregon, and from Harvard College in 1921. Harvard, thereafter, became an integral part of his life. Prior to his retirement in 1963, McCord spent well over forty years at the university, serving in many capacities, principally as alumni editor and fund-raiser. In 1956 Harvard conferred on him its first honorary Doctor of Humane Letters degree.

In 1983 Simmons College in Boston, Massachusetts, presented him with a Doctor of Children's Literature degree; in 1987 Tufts University in Boston awarded him his fourteenth honorary degree. And annually, since 1985, Framingham State College in Framingham, Massachusetts, holds the David McCord Children's Literature Festival.

In the filmstrip *David McCord* in the First Choice: Poets and Poetry series (Pied Piper Productions) he discusses his life and work, treating viewers to an incredible reading of his work. A workshop lesson with the poet suggests two topics for writing a poem—a conversation between inanimate objects and being a seagull or an eagle.

McCord has said, "Poetry is rhythm, just as the planet Earth is rhythm; the best writing, poetry or prose—no matter what the message it conveys—depends on a very sure and subtle rhythm. Good poems for children are never trivial; they are never written without the characteristic chill and fever of a dedicated man at work; children must never hear the stigma of 'I am adult, you are a child.'"

Today, the wondrous rhythm of McCord's work rings as loud as it ever has.

As Myra Cohn Livingston stated in "David McCord: The Singer, the Song, and the Sung" (*The Horn Book*,

February 1979): "Surely, David McCord is the singer whose songs will be sung as long as there are children to listen."

Listen, children. Listen!

## MCCORD TITLES CITED

(All Little, Brown)

*Far and Few, Rhymes of the Never Was and Always Is.*
Illustrated by Henry B. Kane, 1952.

*One at a Time: His Collected Poems for the Young.* Illustrated by Henry B. Kane, 1977.

*Speak Up: More Rhymes of the Never Was and Always Is.*
Illustrated by Marc Simont, 1980.

## ADDITIONAL REFERENCES

Hopkins, Lee Bennett. *Pauses: Autobiographical Reflections of 101 Creators of Children's Books.* Harper, 1995.

Livingston, Myra Cohn, editor. *Poems for Grandmothers.*
Holiday House, 1990.

# EVE MERRIAM

*"What*

*can*

*a*

*poem*

*do?*

*Just*

*about*

*everything."*

EVE MERRIAM was a poet, playwright, and theater director who wrote for all ages. Her play *The Club* received a 1976 Obie Award, the Off-Broadway equivalent of the Tony Award. Most of her poetry for adults focuses on her lifelong major interests—social and political satire and the status of women in modern society.

Feminism was an early and recurring theme in her works, including "We the Women," a program she wrote for CBS television that was the first network documentary on women's rights, and "Out of Our Father's House," a portrayal of prominent American women that was presented at the White House in 1978 and shown on public television's *Great Performances* series.

Merriam was born in Germantown, a suburb of Philadelphia, Pennsylvania, on July 19, 1916, the youngest child of Russian-born parents who owned a chain of women's dress shops.

"I remember growing up surrounded by beautiful birch trees, dogwood trees, and rock gardens. I enjoyed watching birds and just walking through the woods. My mother always had a great feeling for nature and gardening. I probably inherited it from her," she commented.

Books and reading were an important part of her growing-up years; the written word captivated her from a young age.

"Growing up, my brother and I were taken to Gilbert and Sullivan operettas, and we used to change all those tongue-twisting verses of Gilbert's. We would also read aloud great declaiming things like 'Gunga Din' or 'The Highwayman.'"

In my book *Pauses* she continues:

*While I was a student I had my poetry published in various school publications. I began studying at Columbia . . . for my master's degree, but one day, while taking a walk across the George Washington Bridge, I decided not to walk back to Columbia. I quit my studies and decided to find a job. It seemed like a good idea—but what could a poet do? I remembered reading somewhere that Carl Sandburg once worked in advertising, so I would, too. I got a job as an advertising copywriter on Madison Avenue and progressed to become a fashion editor for glamour magazines.*

Her first book of adult poetry, *Family Circle*, published in 1946, won the Yale Younger Poets Prize. She continued to write poetry as well as articles, essays, and biographies; her first book for children, published in 1952, was titled *The Real Book About Franklin Delano Roosevelt.*

Poetry became a passion for her. On the craft of writing she commented, "You can write poems because you must write them; because you can't live your life without writing them. I've spent weeks looking for precisely the right word. It's like having a small marble in your pocket, you can just feel it. Sometimes you find a word and say, 'No, I don't think this is it.' Then you discard it, and take another and another until you get it right. I do think poetry is great fun. That's what I'd like to stress more than anything else; the joy of the sounds of language. What can a poem do? Just about everything."

One can even "eat a poem," as she tells us in one of her classic oft-anthologized works, "How to Eat a Poem," which first appeared in *It Doesn't Always Have to Rhyme.*

Among Merriam's popular collections for younger readers are *Halloween A B C, Higgle Wiggle, A Poem for a Pickle, You Be Good & I'll Be Night,* and *Chortles,* a volume of forty-seven new and selected wordplay poems.

But the one book she was the most impassioned about was *The Inner City Mother Goose,* written in 1969. It is a book of incredible parody, using familiar Mother Goose rhymes to depict the woes of modern times—inadequate housing, unemployment, police corruption, crime and violence in the streets. Although published as an adult book, it soon became popular with all ages and became the basis for the 1971 Broadway musical *Inner City.* After it was out of print, Merriam privately printed one thousand copies of a new edition, which she gave away as a tie-in to a second musical production, *Street Dreams,* which was performed in San Francisco, Chicago, and New York City.

From the time of its first publication, which *Library Journal* called a "little powder keg," *The Inner City Mother Goose* became one of the most consistently banned books in the United States.

In 1996, almost thirty years later, the book was reissued with an introduction by Nikki Giovanni and ten full-color paintings by Caldecott Medalist David Diaz.

Merriam always had refreshing views on the topic of poetry for children. In 1981, the year she received the National Council of Teachers of English (NCTE) Award for Excellence in Poetry for Children, she offered advice to aspiring poets of all ages in "Profile: Eve Merriam" by Glenna Sloan (*Language Arts,* November/

December 1981): "Read a lot. Sit down with anthologies and decide which poems please you. Copy out your favorites in your own handwriting. Buy a notebook and jot down images and descriptions. Be specific; use all the senses. Use your whole body as you write. It might even help sometimes to stand up and move with your words. Don't be afraid of copying a form or a convention, especially in the beginning. And, to give yourself scope and flexibility, remember: It doesn't *always* have to rhyme."

In 1990, during an NCTE program where we appeared together, she firmly stated: "There are a few rules I have for using poetry."

As the audience scrambled to take notes, she bellowed, "*No* rules!"

Two of her popular poems became single-edition picture books in 1995: *Bam Bam Bam*, illustrated with graphics by Dan Yaccarino, and *Train Leaves the Station*, a counting rhyme, illustrated by Dale Gottlieb. In 1998 her delightful verse *What in the World?* appeared as a flap book, illustrated by Barbara J. Phillips-Duke.

On the filmstrip *Eve Merriam* in the First Choice: Poets and Poetry series (Pied Piper Productions) she shows students how to have fun with words. Part Two of the filmstrip offers a dual workshop lesson—one, an introduction to nonsense words, identifying and using them in a poem; two, an introduction of comparisons via the use of similes. Included are a teachers' guide, a photograph, brief biographical information, and ten poems selected from various books.

Merriam died on April 11, 1992, at the age of seventy-five, at St. Vincent's Hospital in Greenwich Village—down the street from where she lived at 102 West 12th Street.

In a moving obituary, Peter Stone and David E. Levine, respectively president and executive director of the Dramatists Guild Council, and Ruth Goetz, president of the Dramatists Guild Fund, wrote:

> *She was our poet of the Inner City and of our forgotten poor, our sleepers-on-sidewalks, our hungry wherever they held out their hands. Her taste and distinction covered over the desperation and fury with which she looked on our brothers and sisters, and made us look at them, and feel for them. Her* Inner City Mother Goose *is a classic of modern American writing and she herself was a classic woman of talent, feeling and tenderness.*

She would have smiled, proudly, over this.

### MERRIAM TITLES CITED

*Bam Bam Bam.* Illustrated by Dan Yaccarino. Henry Holt, 1995; also in paperback.

*Chortles: New and Selected Wordplay Poems.* Illustrated by Sheila Hamanaka. Morrow, 1989.

*Family Circle.* Yale University Press, 1946.

*Halloween A B C.* Illustrated by Lane Smith. Macmillan,
1987; also in paperback.

*Higgle Wiggle: Happy Rhymes.* Illustrated by Hans Wilhelm.
Morrow, 1994; also in paperback.

*Inner City Mother Goose, The,* revised edition. Illustrated by
David Diaz. Simon & Schuster, 1996.

*It Doesn't Always Have to Rhyme.* Illustrated by Malcolm
Spooner. Atheneum, 1964.

*Poem for a Pickle, A: Funnybone Verses.* Illustrated by Sheila
Hamanaka. Morrow, 1989.

*Real Book About Franklin Delano Roosevelt, The.* Illustrated
by Bette J. Davis. Garden City Books, 1952.

*Train Leaves the Station.* Illustrated by Dale Gottlieb. Henry
Holt, 1992.

*What in the World?* Illustrated by Barbara J. Phillips-Duke.
HarperCollins, 1998.

*You Be Good & I'll Be Night: Jump-on-the-Bed Poems.*
Illustrated by Karen Lee Schmidt. Morrow, 1988; also
in paperback.

## ADDITIONAL REFERENCE

Hopkins, Lee Bennett. *Pauses: Autobiographical Reflections of
101 Creators of Children's Books.* Harper, 1995.

# LILIAN MOORE

*"Poems*
*should be*
*like*
*fireworks . . .*
*ready*
*to*
*explode. . . ."*

IN 1997, three decades after the publication of her first book of poetry for children, *I Feel the Same Way*, Lilian Moore, at the age of eighty-eight, published *Poems Have Roots*, seventeen poems with accompanying notes that take readers on unforgettable journeys in which a woodchuck converses with a wren, a deer dreams, and a river doesn't have to die.

Moore was born in New York City on March 17, 1909—St. Patrick's Day. She attended public schools in New York City, went to Hunter College, and did graduate work at Columbia University, both of which are also in New York City.

"I studied Elizabethan literature," she recalled. "I

wanted to teach Christopher Marlowe to college freshman!"

She began teaching in her native city and, due to her expertise in working with children who could not read, became a staff member of the Bureau of Educational Research. There she worked in reading clinics, wrote professional materials, trained teachers, and researched the reading problems of elementary-school children. During this time she began writing for children.

"I had been identified for a long time with what are called easy-to-read materials," Moore wrote of her early work. "It's true I learned from the children the basic difference between dense and open material, but I never understood why people thought that easy-to-read material for children had to be clunky and dull. As an editor, I found out later that what I sensed was true; writers often use too many words. On their way to independence in reading, young children often need easy material, sometimes for only a very short time."

In 1957 she became the first editor of the Arrow Book Club at Scholastic, pioneering the development of the club for readers in grades four through six.

"This was one of the most satisfying things I ever did, helping to launch the *first* quality paperback book program for elementary-school children throughout the United States. . . . Whatever I may have contributed to this program was due in part to my almost total recall of the children I had known and taught. They seemed to haunt me and were specters at my side, vigorously approving or disapproving books we chose for them. And even today, after so many years, I feel so lucky to have had a job I loved so much."

Another of her important contributions to literature was her effort during the late 1960s in forming the International Council on Interracial Books for Children, an organization she helped pioneer.

"I had always tried to encourage minority writers and illustrators," she said. "When the Council was finally formed, it became a conscience of the children's book world."

Moore commented on her first book of poetry, *I Feel the Same Way*: "I think I wrote most of the poems on my way to work each morning. I think of them as my subway songs. Often when I seemed to be staring vacantly at subway ads, I was working intensely on a new idea. Sometimes when it didn't come off, I put it to bed at night, with a profound faith in my unconscious where the special truth I'm seeking usually begins.

"As I worked on the poems, I found myself getting in touch with my own childhood memories, reliving every feeling."

After years of living and working in New York, she moved with her new husband, Sam Reavin, to a farm in upstate New York. After his death she gave up the farm and moved to the West Coast.

"I loved farm life," she recalled. "I had the best of both worlds. I grew up in an exciting city and ended up on a farm. From time to time, Sam, an ex-farmer, wrote children's books, and I, a born and bred ex-city woman, drove a tractor.

"Living in the Hudson Valley, we fought for the preservation to save the Hudson River from pollution. 'A River Doesn't Have to Die,' in *Poems Have Roots*, stems from my life in New York State."

Now out of print, *Sam's Place*, a book of twenty exceptionally crafted poems, describes over a year's time the beauty of the natural world in the Shawangunk Mountains near the farm she grew to love.

In 1988 Moore wrote the short novel *I'll Meet You at the Cucumbers*, a variant of the country–city mouse fable, telling of two country mice, Adam and Junius, who go for a visit to the city so Adam can finally meet his pen pal, Amanda Mouse. Throughout the enchanting novel she wove brief poems from the works of Langston Hughes, Judith Thurman, Carl Sandburg, and Valerie Worth, as well as several newly written poems of her own.

*Don't Be Afraid, Amanda*, a sequel, and *Adam Mouse's Book of Poems*, a collection of thirty verses, appeared in 1992.

A return to writing for the very young came about in 1995 in *I Never Did That Before*, a picture book of fourteen poems illustrated by Lillian Hoban.

About poetry Moore wrote, "Poems should be like fireworks, picked carefully and artfully, ready to explode with unpredictable effects."

In 1985 Moore became the seventh recipient of the National Council of Teachers of English (NCTE) Award for Excellence in Poetry for Children.

At one time Moore sent me a set of galleys of her forthcoming book *Poems Have Roots*. On it was a succinct note: "Friendships have roots, too! Fondly, Lilian."

My roots are richer for knowing Lilian Moore and her contributions to the world of children's literature. Yours will be too!

## MOORE TITLES CITED

(All Atheneum)

*Adam Mouse's Book of Poems*. Illustrated by Kathleen Gary McCord. 1992.

*Don't Be Afraid, Amanda*. Illustrated by Kathleen Gary McCord. 1992.

*I Feel the Same Way*. Illustrated by Robert Quackenbush. 1969.

*I Never Did That Before: Poems*. Illustrated by Lillian Hoban. 1995.

*I'll Meet You at the Cucumbers*. Illustrated by Sharon Wooding. 1988.

*Poems Have Roots: New Poems*. Illustrated by Tad Hills.1997.

*Sam's Place: Poems from the Country*. Illustrated by Talivaldis Stubis. 1973.

# JACK PRELUTSKY

*"A good*
*poem*
*is*
*delicious—*
*as*
*delicious*
*as a*
*chocolate-chip*
*cookie!"*

J ACK PRELUTSKY, prolific writer of light verse, was born in Brooklyn, New York, on September 8, 1940. He attended New York City public schools and graduated from the High School of Music and Art, where he studied voice. After a brief period at Hunter College in New York City, he decided to quit his studies to "do his own thing."

While working in a Greenwich Village music store, he began to fill up long hours drawing imaginary animals, strictly for his own amusement.

"After about six painstaking months, I had created

about two dozen creatures never before seen on this earth," he said. "While leafing through them one evening, I suddenly and inexplicably decided that they needed little poems to accompany them. I don't really know why that thought popped into my head, as I had previously never considered writing, and had in fact flunked freshman English more than once.

"Anyhow, it took me about two hours to compose two dozen little verses, one per critter. I figured that since they took so little effort, they couldn't possibly be any good. I put them aside and forgot about them for several weeks. They were certainly not intended for publication, and in fact I hoped that no one else would see them. However, one evening a close friend who had written several children's books noticed them on my desk and urged me to show them to his publisher. I did so and was astonished to learn from his editor, Susan Carr Hirschman, that I had a genuine talent for verse. She hated my drawings, but I had at last found my medium."

Hirschman not only encouraged him but took him under her wing. As he had no money for food and was about to be evicted from his apartment for not being able to pay rent, she arranged an advance payment for his first book. In addition, she took him to lunch once a week in Macmillan's corporate dining room—but only with the agreement that he'd bring her one poem to each lunch.

Eventually, in 1967, *A Gopher in a Garden* was published and Prelutsky was on his way to becoming one of the most popular writers of light verse in the country.

The list of jobs he held prior to his career as a writer is diverse: cabdriver, busboy, photographer, furniture mover, potter, and folksinger. As a tenor he has performed with several opera companies and choruses; as an actor he has appeared in the musical *Fiddler on the Roof*.

Since *Gopher* he has penned a considerable body of work, including *Circus*, *Nightmares*, *The Headless Horseman Rides Tonight*, and *Tyrannosaurus Was a Beast*, all illustrated by the Caldecott Medalist Arnold Lobel; and four volumes of holiday verse: *It's Christmas*, *It's Halloween*, *It's Thanksgiving*, and *It's Valentine's Day*.

Three of his best-selling larger collections are *The New Kid on the Block*, *Something Big Has Been Here*, and *A Pizza the Size of the Sun*.

In 1993 he teamed up with illustrator Peter Sis to create *The Dragons Are Singing Tonight*.

"When I was a boy, I wasn't able to have a pet," he wrote in *Instructor* magazine (September 1993). "My mother had asthma and she was allergic to practically anything with fur. . . . I had a wild imagination, and often thought about what it would be like to have an exotic pet. . . . I even imagined that I had a dragon!"

Recalling these thoughts, he wrote "I Wish I Had a Dragon," one of seventeen verses in the collection.

Three years later Prelutsky and Sis produced *Monday's Trolls*, a book of seventeen more verses.

As an anthologist he has collected verse for a number

of volumes, among them *The Random House Book of Poetry*, *Read-Aloud Rhymes for the Very Young*, and *The Beauty of the Beast*, a collection of more than two hundred poems about animals.

Despite an adulthood immersed in verse, Prelutsky was not always comfortable with poetry.

"I was an urban child growing up in the Bronx, New York," he said. "I didn't want to hear poems about the village blacksmith; I wanted to hear poems about garage mechanics, about kids like myself, my friends, outer space, or sports. When I discovered poetry in my twenties, I decided I would write about things that kids really cared about, and that I would make poetry delightful.

"Good poetry for children is simple, universal, accessible, and direct. It does what children do—tells you something, then stops; there's no wandering. It catches your heart or your mind. I like to tell children that a good poem is delicious—as delicious as a chocolate-chip cookie!"

Prelutsky can be heard performing many of his works on audiocassettes available from Listening Library; among them are *The Dragons Are Singing Tonight*, *Monday's Trolls*, *The New Kid on the Block*, and *Something Big Has Been Here*.

A twenty-two-minute videocassette, "Meet Jack Prelutsky," is available from American School Publishers. The program will delight students as they watch him perform before an elementary-school audience and reminisce about his childhood and later life, see his home in Olympia, Washington, and learn how arduous it can be to create verse from an idea to a finished form.

In a promotion piece for Greenwillow he wrote:

> . . . *I daydream in my easy chair, and wave my pencil in the air,*
> *Then do what I most love to do, write silly poems just for you.*

Readers who want to chuckle now and then—and who doesn't?—will be glad to know Prelutsky might be sitting, and writing—just for them!

## PRELUTSKY TITLES CITED

*Beauty of the Beast, The: Poems from the Animal Kingdom.* Selected by Jack Prelutsky. Illustrated by Meilo So. Knopf, 1997.

*Circus.* Illustrated by Arnold Lobel. Macmillan, 1974; also in paperback.

*Dragons Are Singing Tonight, The.* Illustrated by Peter Sis. Greenwillow, 1993.

*Gopher in a Garden, A, and Other Animal Poems.* Illustrated by Robert Leydenfrost. Macmillan, 1967.

*Headless Horseman Rides Tonight, The: More Poems to Trouble Your Sleep.* Illustrated by Arnold Lobel. Greenwillow, 1980; also in paperback.

*It's Christmas.* Illustrated by Marylin Hafner. Greenwillow, 1981; also in paperback.

*It's Halloween.* Illustrated by Marylin Hafner. Greenwillow, 1977.

*It's Thanksgiving.* Illustrated by Marylin Hafner. Greenwillow, 1982.

*It's Valentine's Day.* Illustrated by Yossi Abolafia. Greenwillow, 1983; also in paperback.

*Monday's Trolls.* Illustrated by Peter Sis. Greenwillow, 1996.

*New Kid on the Block, The: Poems.* Illustrated by James Stevenson. Greenwillow, 1984.

*Nightmares: Poems to Trouble Your Sleep.* Illustrated by Arnold Lobel. Greenwillow, 1976; also in paperback.

*Pizza the Size of the Sun, A: Poems.* Illustrated by James Stevenson. Greenwillow, 1996.

*Random House Book of Poetry for Children, The.* Selected by Jack Prelutsky. Illustrated by Arnold Lobel. Random House, 1983.

*Read-Aloud Poems for the Very Young.* Selected by Jack Prelutsky. Illustrated by Marc Brown. Knopf, 1986.

*Something Big Has Been Here.* Illustrated by James Stevenson. Greenwillow, 1990.

*Tyrannosaurus Was a Beast: Dinosaur Poems.* Illustrated by Arnold Lobel. Greenwillow, 1988; also in paperback.

# CARL SANDBURG

*"Poetry is*
*an echo*
*asking a*
*shadow dancer*
*to be a*
*partner."*

I N 1982 I HAD THE PRIVILEGE of compiling *Rainbows Are Made*, seventy poems by Carl Sandburg selected from his *Complete Poems*. The book, one of the last to be illustrated by Fritz Eichenberg, a world-renowned lithographer and wood engraver, received a host of awards, including a 1982 *New York Times* choice for Best Illustrated Books. Creating the volume was a highlight of my career—a personal tribute to a man whose work I have long used with children of all ages and whom I so admire.

Born on January 6, 1878, in Galesburg, Illinois, a city about 145 miles southwest of Chicago, in Abraham Lincoln country, Sandburg was the son of poor Swedish immigrants. His father was a railroad blacksmith. Sandburg was eleven years old when he began to combine school and work. After the eighth grade he left school altogether. He drove a milk wagon, helped in a barber shop, waited at a lunch counter, and worked as a farm-hand, a laborer on the railroad, a secretary, a newspaper reporter, a political organizer, a historian, a lecturer, and a collector and singer of folk songs. He frequently toured the United States; with guitar in hand, he sang folk songs and recited his poems.

His first published poetry for adults, *In Reckless Ecstasy*, appeared in 1904. Fifty copies were printed by his professor, Phillip Green Wright, who owned and operated a printing press in Galesburg. Three additional volumes of his work were also printed by Wright between 1907 and 1910.

In 1914 Harriet Monroe, editor of the avant-garde *Poetry: A Magazine of Verse*, received a group of nine poems by Sandburg. They shocked her. They were unlike anything she was used to reading and/or receiving. She published all nine in the magazine, including his famous free verse "Chicago."

Sandburg's first major work, *Chicago Poems*, appeared two years later from Henry Holt. Following this volume, Sandburg's writings were published at a rapid pace reflecting the tempo, life, and language of the people he encountered.

He once said, "I glory in this world of men and women torn with troubles, yet living on to love and laugh through it all."

His first book for children, *Early Moon*, appeared in 1930, a collection of poems culled from his various adult books. A second book for young readers, *Wind Song*, also culled from his adult works, was published in 1960. *Early Moon* begins with his must-read "Short Talk on Poetry," a beautiful essay explaining "how little anybody knows about poetry, how it is made, what it is made of, how long men and women have been making it, where it came from, when it began, who started it and why, and who knows all about it."

Thirty years of Sandburg's life were spent preparing the monumental six-volume biography of Abraham Lincoln; in 1940 he was awarded the Pulitzer Prize in History of the United States for the last four volumes, *Abraham Lincoln: The War Years*. In 1951 he received a second Pulitzer Prize, in Poetry, for his *Complete Poems*.

Works by Sandburg appear in nearly every major anthology of poetry. His words are as fresh today as they were decades ago and will continue to be years hence.

In the late 1990s a never-before-published poem of Sandburg's was found. The poem is the basis of the picture book *Not Everyday an Aurora Borealis for Your Birthday*, illustrated by Caldecott Honor recipient Anita Lobel. The year 1998 marked the publication of *Grassroots*, illustrated by Wendell Minor, a tribute to Sandburg's work reflecting the Midwest.

Sandburg's birthplace, 331 East 3rd Street in

Galesburg, stands as a monument to the poet. In 1968 Connemara Farm, where he spent his last years, became a national historic site, administered by the National Park Service. Located five miles from Hendersonville, North Carolina, the home and grounds are open to the public. The entire house is exactly as it was when Sandburg lived there. Each year thousands of adults and children visit these memorials.

A biography for adult readers, *Carl Sandburg*, by Penelope Niven, is based upon more than 50,000 papers in the Sandburg Collection at Connemara.

The poet died on July 22, 1967, at the age of eighty-nine. Upon his death at Connemara, President Lyndon Baines Johnson issued this statement:

*Carl Sandburg needs no epitaph. It is written for all times in the fields, the cities, the face and heart of the land he loved and the people he celebrated and inspired. With the world we mourn his passing. It is our pride and fortune as Americans that we will always hear Carl Sandburg's voice within ourselves. For he gave us the truest and most enduring vision of our own greatness.*

The rainbow maker's voice *will* forever be heard.

## SANDBURG TITLES CITED

*Abraham Lincoln: The War Years.* Harcourt, 1939.
*Chicago Poems.* Henry Holt, 1916.
*Complete Poems of Carl Sandburg: Revised and Expanded*

*Edition.* Harcourt, 1970.

*Early Moon.* Illustrated by James Daugherty. Harcourt, 1930.

*Grassroots: Poems by Carl Sandburg.* Illustrated by Wendell Minor. Browndeer, 1998.

*In Reckless Ecstasy.* Privately printed, 1904.

*Not Everyday an Aurora Borealis for Your Birthday: A Love Poem.* Illustrated by Anita Lobel. Knopf, 1998.

*Rainbows Are Made: Poems by Carl Sandburg.* Selected by Lee Bennett Hopkins. Illustrated by Fritz Eichenberg. Harcourt, 1982; also in paperback.

*Wind Song.* Illustrated by William A. Smith. Harcourt, 1960.

## ADDITIONAL REFERENCE

Niven, Penelope. *Carl Sandburg: A Biography.* Scribner's, 1991.

# SHEL SILVERSTEIN

*"I would hope
that people,
no matter
what age,
would find
something
to identify with
in my books."*

WITH ANY GROUP OF CHILDREN—anywhere—all I have to do is mention the name Shel Silverstein and many immediately cry out, "Read 'Sarah Cynthia Sylvia Stout Who Would Not Take the Garbage Out'"; or "Read 'Jimmy Jet and His TV Set.'" If today's children know of light verse, they *know* Shel Silverstein.

Author-illustrator Shelby Silverstein, born in Chicago, Illinois, in 1932, has had a diverse career. During the 1950s, while he was a G.I. in Japan, his early cartoons appeared in *Stars and Stripes*, a periodical produced by the armed services. Years later he was a regular contributor to *Playboy* magazine, creating cartoons and offbeat verses.

In 1963, when he was thirty-one, his first book for children, *Lafcadio, the Lion Who Shot Back*, an amusing fable, was published. In a rare interview with Jean F. Mercier (*Publishers Weekly*, February 24, 1975), he discussed his writing for children: "I never planned to write or draw for kids. It was Tomi Ungerer, a friend of mine [and a distinguished author-illustrator of children's books], who insisted . . . practically dragged me, kicking and screaming into Ursula Nordstrom's office [she was editor-in-chief of the children's-book department at Harper] and she convinced me that Tomi was right. I could do children's books."

Nordstrom was always right! She published the early work and established the careers of hundreds of authors and illustrators, including Ruth Krauss, Maurice Sendak, Charlotte Zolotow, E. B. White, and Garth Williams.

Following *Lafcadio, the Lion Who Shot Back*, a steady output of Silverstein's best-selling books appeared, including *The Giving Tree* and *A Giraffe and a Half*.

In 1974 *Where the Sidewalk Ends* established him as one of America's most popular writers of light verse. *A Light in the Attic* appeared in 1981, selling more than 575,000 copies within the first year of publication. In 1985 the book's sales broke publishing industry records, staying on *The New York Times*' best-seller list for 182 weeks—longer than any hardcover book in the list's fifty-year-plus history. Some of the awards Silverstein has acquired include the 1984 Children's Book Award for nonfiction from the New Jersey Library Association and, in the same year, the William Allen White Award, voted upon by more than 52,000 fourth- through eighth-grade children throughout the state of Kansas—the first book of verse to win the William Allen White Award in the program's thirty-two-year history.

Both *A Light in the Attic* and *Where the Sidewalk Ends* have sold close to fifteen million hardcover copies and have been translated into more than twenty languages.

In 1996 Silverstein published *Falling Up*. Within months of its publication the book sold more than 300,000 copies.

A very private person, Silverstein has long refused to discuss his books or even allow HarperCollins to release any photographs or biographical information. He divides his time among places from coast to coast.

In addition to his books for children and adults, he is also a noted composer, lyricist, folksinger, and performer. One of his most popular songs, "A Boy Named Sue," was recorded by Johnny Cash. His country-western offering "I'm Checkin' Out (of the Heartbreak Hotel)," performed by Meryl Streep in the film *Postcards from the Edge*, was nominated for an Academy Award for Best Song of 1990.

He is also the author of several plays, including his first, *The Lady or the Tiger* (1981), *The Crate* (1985), and *Oh, Hell* (1989).

Film buffs can catch his appearance in the 1971 film *Who Is Harry Kellerman and Why Is He Saying Those*

*Terrible Things About Me?*, starring Dustin Hoffman. In 1988, with playwright David Mamet, he coauthored the motion picture *Things Change*, starring Don Ameche.

"I would hope that people, no matter what age, would find something to identify with in my books," he comments. "Pick one up and experience a personal sense of discovery."

In *Climb into the Bell Tower* Myra Cohn Livingston wrote:

> *Silverstein's genius lies . . . in finding a new way to present moralism, beguiling his child readers with a technique that establishes him as both an errant, mischievous, and inventive child as well as an understanding, trusted, and wise adult. . . .*
>
> *What he says in light verse and drawing to children is of such importance, such urgency that we must be grateful that over five million copies of [*Where the Sidewalk Ends* and *A Light in the Attic*] alone are being read. In a world that needs a generation of imaginative thinkers, may there be millions and millions more!*

Undoubtedly there will be!

## SILVERSTEIN TITLES CITED

(All published by Harper)
*Falling Up.* 1996.
*Giraffe and a Half, A.* 1964.
*Giving Tree, The.* 1964.

*Lafcadio, the Lion Who Shot Back.* 1963.
*Light in the Attic, A.* 1981.
*Where the Sidewalk Ends: Poems and Drawings.* 1974.

## ADDITIONAL REFERENCE

Livingston, Myra Cohn. *Climb into the Bell Tower: Essays on Poetry.* Harper, 1990.

# VALERIE WORTH

*"Never let*
*the mud puddle*
*get lost*
*in poetry—*
*because*
*in many ways*
*the mud puddle*
*is*
*the*
*poetry."*

WHEN I CHAIRED the 1991 National Council of Teachers of English (NCTE) Award for Excellence in Poetry for Children, the committee came to a unanimous decision that Valerie Worth would be honored as the ninth recipient. At the time Worth was too ill to accept the award personally. But she found time to talk with me about her life and work.

She died three years later, on July 31, 1994, at the age of sixty.

Born in Philadelphia, Pennsylvania on October 29,

1933, she grew up in nearby Swarthmore, where her father taught biology at Swarthmore College. In 1947 the family moved to Tampa, Florida, staying for three years. From Florida the Worths moved to India when a dramatic opportunity arose for Worth's father to study malaria there.

Following one year of high school in Bangalore, Worth returned to the United States—back to Swarthmore, where she later graduated with a B.A. degree in English. In college she met a fellow student, George Bahlke; they married shortly after graduation.

Worth's love of literature, especially poetry, was instilled by her parents.

"Both my parents read poetry," she told me. "My father wrote poetry himself—poetry connected to the world of nature and biology. I well remember my mother reading to me, but it was her *choice* of reading that had great influence on my life. Her enthusiasm for fine literature and art was a force for me—a force that would last a lifetime.

"Although I loved reading poetry as a child, something in me felt unsatisfied, as if something more could be done with it. When I turned to writing, I tried to create what I wanted when I was a child—a poetry that would read more deeply into the world I saw around me."

After writing for adults, including poetry that appeared in magazines such as *Harper's*, she turned to writing what she termed "small poems." For four or five years she submitted them to publishers, but there was little interest in them.

When her husband finished his Ph.D. degree at Yale University (where she worked as a secretary in the promotion department at Yale University Press), they lived in Virginia, New Jersey, and Vermont, finally settling in Clinton, New York, where he taught at Kirkland College. Joining an informal writing group, Worth met the well-known Newbery Honor–winning author and illustrator Natalie Babbitt, wife of Samuel Fisher Babbitt, the first president of Kirkland.

"I read some of my poems aloud to the group. When Natalie heard them, she said, 'I'd like to send your poems to Michael di Capua at Farrar, Straus & Giroux to look at.' The whole experience was a fortuitous one."

Shortly after her work reached di Capua, he offered to publish her first volume, *Small Poems*.

"This was a great time for me," she said. "I had been writing for so long and I wasn't publishing much."

Knowing that an illustrator was being sought to do pictures for the collection, she asked Babbitt if *she* might have any interest in illustrating the book.

"I'm so glad you asked me!" exclaimed Babbitt.

Thus the collaboration began; the team went on to work on five more volumes together.

*Small Poems* appeared in 1972, followed by *More Small Poems*, *Still More Small Poems*, *Small Poems Again*,

*All the Small Poems*, and *All the Small Poems and Fourteen More*, published in 1994.

Within these six volumes Worth has given readers a total of 113 small poems, ranging in subjects from autumn geese to zinnias. Her poems are sharp, solid, eloquent evocations of utilitarian objects in which she brings new, dramatic life to the unexpected. Her crystal-clear vision causes us to see the everyday world in fresh, insightful, larger-than-life ways. Amoebas, anteaters, tractors, and telephone poles—each subject springs, rings to new heights via her perfect creations.

Lilian Moore, a friend of Worth's, wrote in the article "A Second Look" (*The Horn Book*, July/August 1988): "These are not small poems, any more than the little stitched 'packets' that Emily Dickinson left behind were small poems. What we have in [Worth's work] is an unusual resource—an opportunity to share with children real poetry about the real world, to take them, as it were, on a field trip with special binoculars."

Worth commented to me: "I write about what is vivid, exciting, magical to me—about the way I see things now, or how I viewed them as a child—or a combination of both child/adult feelings. I write about things that strike a chord in me, be it a lawnmower or a kaleidoscope or coat hangers.

"I have strong responses to what finds its way into my work. What I have tried to do in many of my poems for children is to re-create in verbal form the nonverbal experiences of childhood. Of course some children (as well as some adults) simply have no interest in such translations; but in spite of all the distractions abounding in our culture, there are surely still some who do have such an interest or would if they received sufficient encouragement. However, much poetry written for children today seems directly *opposed* to the full or subtle experiencing of reality.

"It has always seemed to me that any tree or flower, any living creature, even any old board or brick or bottle, possesses a mysterious poetry of its own; a poetry still wordless, formless, inaudible, but asking to be translated into words and images and sounds—to be expressed as a poem. Perhaps it could be said that written poetry is simply a way of revealing and celebrating the essentially poetic nature of the world itself."

Although a great deal of time and care went into the construction of each of her works, she described the writing process as: "Some of my poems just spring up— full bloom! Others can take days, weeks, months. Usually ideas come first, *then* the poetry takes hold. It is a matter of thought, sound, imagery—all working together in balance to create the effect that I want to convey.

"Then there are times I *know* I am going in a wrong direction. Then I have to pull back—pull back strongly and start all over. My aim is to focus clearly on a subject, pare down words so there can be nothing extraneous in any of my poems."

I asked Worth if she had any advice to offer children who want to write poetry.

She told me: "I would say write poetry for the fun of it, for the joy of it, for the love of it. And especially for the love of the things you write about, whatever they may be. But never forget that the subject is as important as your feelings: The mud puddle itself is as important as your pleasure in looking at it or splashing through it. Never let the mud puddle get lost in the poetry—because in many ways the mud puddle *is* the poetry."

In addition to her small poems she penned *At Christmastime*, a cycle of twenty-eight poems heralding the holiday and the winter-to-spring seasons, illustrated with full-color woodcuts by Antonio Frasconi, and three works of fiction: *Curlicues, The Fortunes of Two Pug Dogs*; *Gypsy Gold*; and *Fox Hill*.

Worth's legacy may seem small, but like fragile snowflakes, the mystery of a spider's spun web, or a tiny rich glistening near a riverbed, her work contains enormous thoughts, evokes huge feelings.

## WORTH TITLES CITED

*All the Small Poems.* Illustrated by Natalie Babbitt. Farrar, Straus, 1987; also in paperback.

*All the Small Poems and Fourteen More.* Illustrated by Natalie Babbitt. Farrar, Straus, 1994; also in paperback.

*At Christmastime.* Illustrated by Antonio Frasconi. Harper, 1992.

*Curlicues, The Fortunes of Two Pug Dogs.* Farrar, Straus, 1980.

*Fox Hill.* Farrar, Straus, 1986.

*Gypsy Gold.* Farrar, Straus, 1983.

*More Small Poems.* Illustrated by Natalie Babbitt. Farrar, Straus, 1976.

*Small Poems.* Illustrated by Natalie Babbitt. Farrar, Straus, 1972.

*Small Poems Again.* Illustrated by Natalie Babbitt. Farrar, Straus, 1986.

*Still More Small Poems.* Illustrated by Natalie Babbitt. Farrar, Straus, 1978.

# JANE YOLEN

*"I think
of poetry
as . . . the
space
between
wingbeats."*

JANE YOLEN is a phenomenon in the world of children's literature. She has produced over 200 books for children and adults, including short stories, novels, plays, picture books, music books, anthologies, essays—and poetry.

Yolen, born on February 11, 1939, in New York City, grew up in a literary environment. Her father, Will Hyatt Yolen, was an author of books and radio scripts; her mother, Isabelle Berlin Yolen, was also a writer and composer of crossword puzzles, many of which appeared in children's magazines.

While in college Yolen wrote poetry and sang folk songs professionally to earn money for living expenses. After receiving a B.A. degree in 1960 from Smith

College, she was a production assistant for *Saturday Review* magazine for six months, followed by a long career in publishing.

In 1963 her first book in rhyme, *See This Little Line?*, appeared. Yolen was off and rhythmically running!

I asked her, "As a multifaceted writer, how do you decide when you are going to do a book in poetic form?"

Her reply came quick, terse: "I don't decide," she said. "I *never* decide. The book decides. I follow!"

Her first two books of poems both appeared in 1980: *Dragon Night* and *How Beastly!* Although *Dragon Night*, a collection of sixteen lullabies a variety of animals might sing to their young, is out of print, several of the verses, such as "Grandpa Bear's Lullaby" and "Caterpillar's Lullaby," have been reprinted in numerous anthologies. *How Beastly!* began her foray into nonsense verse. The book features twenty-two selections of "never were" creatures, including "The Bluffalo," "The Centerpede," and "The Dinosore."

Since the publication of these two volumes, Yolen has created more than twenty books of original poetry and anthologies for readers of all ages, from the playful *The Three Bears Rhyme Book* and *The Three Bears Holiday Rhyme Book* to the elegantly produced young-adult collection *Among Angels*, which she coauthored with Newbery Medalist Nancy Willard.

"What is poetry?" I asked her. "What is poetry to you?"

She replied: "I think of poetry as the soul of literature. It is what we see and hear the moment before sleep takes us. It is the space between wingbeats. The pause between heartbeats. The first touch of the drumstick on the tight stretch of drum hide and the slight burring after.

"Do you know what else it is, Lee? It is: Hard work. A single great line. A word discovered after an afternoon of trying. An emotion caught in the hand, in the mouth. Two words that bump up against one another and create something new. A song between friends. Hard work. *Hard* work. I am never satisfied. I can approximate. And sometimes if I'm lucky, I come pretty close to what I am trying to do.

"Since I write both humorous/light verse and serious poems, I find it difficult to speak about poetry without hedging. I enjoy writing funny poems, and I think children and teachers find those the most accessible. My more serious poetry and, to my mind, better poems are not as easy to discover. What the serious poems tend to have in common is a singability, driven by a line that often ends with a single strong stress syllable. I am, and always have been, quite musical, which informs a great deal of my poetry. I am also an admirer of the bardic and psalmic traditions and often consciously and unconsciously use those rhythms in my work."

The bardic and psalmic traditions she speaks about are seen in her children's books *O Jerusalem* and *Sacred Places*.

*O Jerusalem*, which she wrote in celebration of the

three-thousand-year anniversary of the founding of the city—a holy place for three religions: Judaism, Christianity, and Islam—features fourteen poems with notes. In *Sacred Places* she writes about varied places around the world that are considered sacred by various cultures, including Easter Island, the Mayan temple of Copán, and the Shinto shrine at Itsukushima.

I asked if she had a favorite among her books of poetry.

"Every author has trouble singling out a favorite book or favorite poem," she stated, "but *Ring of Earth* holds a special place in my heart."

*Ring of Earth*, handsomely illustrated by John Wallner, views the four seasons from the perspective of a weasel, spring peeper, dragonfly, and goose.

"Three of my poetic influences are John Donne, William Butler Yeats, and Dylan Thomas. Among my favorite poets for children are David McCord (*the* master), Lilian Moore (who creates little masterpieces and who is a Grand Lady), and Edward Lear," she said.

Mother of three grown children, Yolen lives with her husband, David Stemple, on a farm in western Massachusetts and in St. Andrews, Scotland.

Honors bestowed upon her work are legion, among them the Regina Medal and Kerlan Award for her body of work in children's literature. Her picture book *The Emperor and the Kite*, based on her relationship with her father, who was an international kite-flying champion, provided Ed Young with the text for what became a 1968 Caldecott Honor Book. *Owl Moon*, which stemmed from her husband's interest in birding and sharing the experience with their daughter, received the 1988 Caldecott Medal for the illustrations by John Schoenherr. In 1997, on the tenth anniversary of the book's publication, it was released in paperback.

"Ten years later," Yolen said, "and the little girl in *Owl Moon* has her own little girl. Pa can't wait to take our granddaughter out owling. So we change—but the story remains. I like that about books."

Readers can learn more about her work and life in *A Letter from Phoenix Farm*, a picture-book autobiography illustrated with full-color photographs by her son Jason Stemple.

May the prolific pen of Yolen never, ever run dry!

### YOLEN TITLES CITED

*Among Angels: Poems.* By Jane Yolen and Nancy Willard. Illustrated by S. Saelig Gallagher. Harcourt, 1995.

*Dragon Night and Other Lullabies.* Illustrated by Demi. Methuen, 1980.

*Emperor and the Kite, The.* Illustrated by Ed Young. World, 1967.

*How Beastly! A Menagerie of Nonsense Poems.* Illustrated by James Marshall. Collins, 1980; reissued by Wordsong, 1994.

*Letter from Phoenix Farm, A.* Photographs by Jason Stemple. Owen, 1992.

*O Jerusalem*. Illustrated by John Thompson. Scholastic, 1966.

*Owl Moon*. Illustrated by John Schoenherr. Philomel, 1987; also in paperback.

*Ring of Earth: A Child's Book of Seasons*. Illustrated by John Wallner. Harcourt, 1986.

*Sacred Places*. Illustrated by David Shannon. Harcourt, 1996.

*See This Little Line?* Illustrated by Kathleen Elgin. McKay, 1963.

*Three Bears Holiday Rhyme Book, The*. Illustrated by Jane Dyer. Harcourt, 1995; also in paperback.

*Three Bears Rhyme Book, The*. Illustrated by Jane Dyer. Harcourt, 1987; also in paperback.

# PART THREE

# "And One Day the World Will Know Me"

## SPARKING CHILDREN TO WRITE POETRY

CHILDREN should and can write poetry. Once they are exposed to and begin to enjoy poetry over a period of time, many will compose poems of their own. Children's work is meant to be shared. They can read their verse to one another, print it in a class or school newspaper, print it out on a computer, include it in a play or assembly program, or give it as a priceless gift to someone special.

Often I receive letters from parents, teachers, librarians, and children asking me how to get a child's poem published. The important thing should be the creation of something from within the child—that is enough! A child's poem is not any better because it appears in print. We must not feel that everything a child writes is publisher-bound. One's poems do not have to appear in print to be heard or enjoyed by oneself, one's peers, or an intimate group. We should encourage children to write, play with language, use words in new and special ways, rewrite, and develop their creative potential while having fun creating poetry.

Writing poetry is not easy. Not at all! Established poets describe difficulties with their work over and over again. Valerie Worth, for example, wrote that her poem "Water Lily," which contains ten lines and a total of twenty words, went through almost a hundred revisions before it was published in *All the Small Poems*.

Karla Kuskin, in *Thoughts, Pictures, and Words*, tells readers: "Trying to get a story or poem just the way you want it is hard work. I spend a great deal of time re-writing."

*Poem-Making* by Myra Cohn Livingston offers a wide array of ideas to get middle-grade and older readers involved in creating original poetry.

Both children and adults will enjoy *Knock at a Star*, an anthology of poetry selected by X. J. Kennedy and Dorothy M. Kennedy. More than 160 poems by contemporary and past masters of the art of poetry are included in this volume. The book is divided into four sections to stimulate the reading and writing of poetry. All types of verse are represented—rhyme, free verse, short-verse forms. The last chapter, "Do It Yourself (Writing Your Own Poems)," gives readers ten suggestions for involving children with poetry.

In *For the Good of the Earth and Sun* Georgia Heard

shares her experiences of bringing poetry into the lives of children in New York City public schools. The book describes how she taught children to love poetry and how she encouraged them to discover and unleash their writing potential.

*Sunrises and Songs* by Amy A. McClure relates the author's experiences during a year spent in Mt. Victory, a small rural town in Ohio, visiting the combined fifth- and sixth-grade classrooms of Sheryl Read and Peggy Harrison, teachers who immersed their students in poetry. McClure shows how the children wrote, revised, and refined their own creations. In addition, McClure shares a warm, spirited account of how forty-eight children in this multiage, rural classroom took poetry into their hearts.

There are no doubt many excellent techniques designed to encourage children to write poetry. I believe that in examining with children poetry itself—the rhyme schemes, the literary forms—in an enjoyable and relaxed manner, some amazing poems result.

### SIMILES AND METAPHORS

One way to start children writing is by introducing them to similes and metaphors.

Similes compare one thing to another using words such as *like* or *as*.

Give children the phrase "as green as ——" and ask for an immediate response. When I suggest this at adult workshops, I ask the audience to give *their* response. Immediately a chorus chants, "As green as *grass*!"

Laughingly, I tell the group that if their first-, third-, or sixth-grade youngsters said that, the adults would call them uncreative! Yet this is a perfect response. What is greener than a beautiful patch of grass? To a child "tired answers" are really quite fresh, since every day brings new experiences, new reactions.

Try other similes using fresh subjects, for example, "as big as ——," "as slow as ——," or "as *anything* as."

From the *like* or *as* phrases lead children into other comparisons. "The playground was as —— as ——." "The rainbow was like ——" or "The frog was like ——."

Third graders have responded:

> *The mouse is as small as my hand on the*
> *day I was born.*
> *The giant in the fairy tale is as tall as a*
> *basketball player.*
> *The car wash is as noisy as a hurricane*
> *hurrying by.*

Children of all ages will delight in reading or hearing Norton Juster's *As: A Surfeit of Similes*.

In a short but pointed article, "Age and Grade Expectancy in Poetry: Maturity in Self-Expression" (*Today's Catholic Teacher*, September 12, 1969, pp. 18–19), Nina Willis Walter tells about a child's first attempt at writing poetry using comparison:

> *The comparison of snow to a blanket is not new, but the following poem was a creative effort by the child who wrote it because the idea of making comparison was new to him and because he was looking at the snow and saying what it looked like to him:*
>
> *The snow*
> *Is like a big white blanket*
> *On the ground.*
>
> Joey Barnes, Age 6.

Rather than dismissing Joey's comparison as uncreative, it would be better to develop additional ideas and feelings about snow using other similes. This, then, is a small beginning, a way to start girls and boys thinking in terms of poetic imagery, finally setting their thoughts down via the use of creative language.

Another way to inspire creative writing experiences in children is to introduce them to metaphors.

Metaphors abound in poetry. Share such examples as "Sun" by Valerie Worth in *All the Small Poems*, in which she compares the sun to a leaping fire; or William Shakespeare's "All the world's a stage/And all the men and women in it merely players," from *As You Like It*.

## TRADITIONAL VERSE FORMS

After students have had the experience of learning about and writing similes and metaphors, they can be introduced to various poetic verse forms beginning with basic couplets, tercets, and quatrains, progressing to short verse forms, cinquains, and limericks, and forms that invite wordplay such as parody and concrete poetry.

## COUPLET

The couplet is the simplest and oldest rhyming form; it consists of two lines bound together by rhyme. Couplets have been written for centuries. As early as 1683 couplets were used to teach children both the alphabet and religious morals, emphasizing the sinful nature of humankind. Such rhymes appeared in *The New England Primer*:

> *A—in Adam's fall*
> *We sinned all.*
>
> *Z—Zaccheus he did climb a tree*
> *His Lord to see.*

Many Mother Goose rhymes appear in couplet form:

> *Here am I, Little Jumping Joan;*
> *When nobody's with me, I'm all alone.*
>
> *Jack be nimble, Jack be quick,*
> *Jack jump over the candlestick.*

Students might try writing simple verses in couplet form about holidays, pets, food—anything.

## TERCET

One form of the tercet, or triplet, is a stanza of three lines that uses one end-rhyme sound. An example by Robert Browning is:

*Boot, saddle, to horse, and away!*
*Rescue my castle before the hot day*
*Brightens to blue from its silvery gray.*

## QUATRAIN

The word *quatrain* derives from the French *quatre*, meaning four. The quatrain is written in four lines and can consist of any metrical pattern or rhyme scheme. In Harlem, New York, one fourth grader created a verse that tells a great deal about herself, includes excellent word images, and evokes much thought. The child titled her work "My Seed":

*The seed is growing deep inside*
*It cannot hide, it cannot hide.*
*It shoves and pushes, it bangs and kicks*
*And one day the world will know me.*

Ask children to hunt for examples of quatrains written by master poets and read them to the class. A collection of these can prompt discussion about how much can be said in just four lines. Examples include John Ciardi's "Warning," depicting the dangers of a whirlpool, in *The Man Who Sang the Sillies*; "Yoo-hoo, Mrs. Kangaroo" in Mary Ann Hoberman's *A Fine Fat*

*Pig*; or the Mother Goose rhyme that amusingly sums up the four seasons of the year:

> *Spring is showery, flowery, bowery.*
> *Summer is hoppy, croppy, poppy.*
> *Autumn is wheezy, sneezy, freezy.*
> *Winter is slippy, drippy, nippy.*

See also David McCord's *One at a Time* for a series of quatrains.

### CINQUAIN

Cinquain, a delicately compressed unrhymed stanza, contains twenty-two syllables broken into five lines in a two-four-six-eight-two pattern. The form was originated by Adelaide Crapsey, born on September 9, 1878, in Brooklyn Heights, New York. A detailed account of her life appears in an article I wrote, "From 'Trudeau's Garden'" (*Elementary English*, October 1967, pp. 613–614, 616).

In 1915, a year after her death, a slender collection of her work simply titled *Verse* was published containing cinquains as well as other poetic forms.

Carl Sandburg in *Cornhuskers* (1918, later to appear in *Complete Poems*) wrote a free-verse poem, "Adelaide Crapsey"—a tribute to her life and writings—in which he reminisced, "I read your heart in a book."

In my travels around the country I have introduced this form to many children. Here are several examples of cinquains written by children from New Jersey, New York, and Colorado:

*These are*
*Two happy times—*
*Watching a baseball game,*
*Seeing your baby brother walk*
*Alone.*

*One day*
*A horse ran fast*
*He ran so fast that wind*
*Sunlight, and all the blue of day*
*Flew gone!*

*Dreaming*
*Clouds over head*
*With grass for my soft bed*
*With flowers for a dream pillow*
*I stay.*

Other poems in cinquain form to share with children appear in *Sky Songs* by Myra Cohn Livingston, and in David McCord's *One at a Time*, which offers a five-page lesson on the cinquain form for readers and writers.

Although the cinquain form has been one of the most popular creative-writing assignments given to children, it is also one of the most abused. Textbooks and teachers' guides, as well as journal articles, continue to pass along misinformation about the form, turning it into an exercise in grammar and calling for lists of nouns, adjectives, and participles. A lovely form of poetry, the cinquain deserves our attention and appreciation.

The traditional verse form—whether couplet, tercet, quatrain, or cinquain—can offer both children and adults the opportunity to explore language and rhythm in individual or group setting. But most of all, these forms should offer us all a chance to have a good time with words!

## LIMERICK

Limericks immediately bring to mind the poet Edward Lear, who perfected this form to amuse the grandchildren of his friend the Earl of Derby. The nineteenth-century master of the limerick form wrote many verses, such as:

> There was an Old Man in a tree,
> Whose whiskers were lovely to see;
>> But the birds of the air,
>> Pluck'd them perfectly bare,
> To make themselves nests in that tree.

Since 1846, when Lear's *Book of Nonsense* appeared, his humor has remained timeless.

The form consists of five lines. Lines one, two, and five rhyme; lines three and four may or may not rhyme.

After hearing many limericks written by Lear and others, children will want to create their own. To help them, you might try this: Write one line on the chalkboard—for example, "There was a man with thirty-three cats." Encourage children to make a list of all the words they can think of that rhyme with *cats*. Then they can suggest a second line for the limerick, ending with one of their words. This line is also written on the chalkboard. Next, the children can think of a third line following the thought of the limerick but not ending with a rhyming word. Now they can make a second list of words rhyming with the last word in the third line and use this as a resource to finish line four. Line five can end with a rhyming word from the first list they prepared.

The limerick form gives children an opportunity to use interesting-sounding words, experiment with language, and have fun in clever word ways.

Arnold Lobel's *The Book of Pigericks*, original limericks all about pigs in a beautifully designed volume, can motivate writing lessons based on other animals. Can you just envision a bulletin-board display proudly touting cat-ericks, dog-ericks, horse-ericks—animal-ericks of all kinds—along with children's artwork?

X. J. Kennedy's *Uncle Switch*, a book of "loony limericks," features a most eccentric man involved in a number of zany situations.

In *Lots of Limericks*, selected by Myra Cohn Livingston, you will find many of Edward Lear's rhymes along with others by such notables as John Ciardi and Ogden Nash.

*Knock at a Star* by X. J. Kennedy and Dorothy M.

Kennedy presents an introduction to the form, including examples.

Myra Cohn Livingston's *How Pleasant to Know Mr. Lear!*, a tribute to the humorist, contains a scholarly selection of Lear's story poems, limericks, notes, and artwork, divided into eleven sections. Livingston's introduction describes Lear's life and work. Appended is an informative "Notes on the Sources of the Poems, Further Facts, and Speculations About Old Derry Down Derry," plus an index of titles and first lines.

## PARODY

A great deal of writing fun can be had by showing children how to experiment with parody. Limericks and Mother Goose rhymes are popular forms to use to introduce parody. Why not have children set some of the Mother Goose rhymes in an amusement park, as Hollywood or television personalities, or at the seashore? One fourth grader offered:

> *Little Boy Blue, come blow your horn.*
> *The sheep's in the meadow, the cow's in the corn.*
> *Where is the boy that looks after the sheep?*
> *He's down at the seashore buying hot dogs cheap.*

A fifth grader came up with:

> *There was an old woman*
> *Who lived in a shoe,*

*She had so many children . . .*
*That she looked in the Yellow Pages*
*And called a Real Estate Man.*

Middle-grade and high-school-aged readers will find inspiration in Eve Merriam's treasure trove of parody, *The Inner City Mother Goose*.

Ellyn Roe, a teacher at Cedar Heights Junior High School in Port Orchard, Washington, uses Elizabeth Barrett Browning's sonnet "How do I love thee? Let me count the ways . . ." with her students on Valentine's Day. First she reads the piece aloud, giving students the chance to offer interpretations of lines they find difficult. Students then use the first line and proceed to list attributes of a beloved person or object. One example is:

*How do I love thee? Let me count the ways.*
*I love the way thee runs to greet me after school.*
*I love the way thy coat gleams in the afternoon sun*
*As I run my fingers through its furry softness. . . .*

Other examples of parodies can be found in *Knock at a Star* by X. J. Kennedy and Dorothy M. Kennedy.

Lewis Carroll was a master of parody, and both *Alice's Adventures in Wonderland* and *Through the Looking-Glass* abound in parodies. For example, the theologian Dr. Isaac Watts had written several four-line stanzas, "Against Idleness and Mischief," published in 1715 in *Divine Songs Attempted in Early Language, for Use of Children*.

*How doth the little busy Bee*
*Improve each shining Hour,*
*And gather Honey all the Day*
*From ev'ry op'ning Flow'r!*

*How skillfully she builds her Cell!*
*How neat she spreads the Wax;*
*And labours hard to store it well*
*With the sweet Food she makes.*

In *Alice's Adventures in Wonderland* Lewis Carroll turned this into:

*How doth the little crocodile*
*Improve his shining tail*
*And pour the waters of the Nile*
*On every golden scale.*

*How cheerfully he seems to grin,*
*How neatly spreads his claws,*
*And welcomes little fishes in*
*With gently smiling jaws!*

The wonderful verse beginning "You are old, Father William," in *Alice's Adventures in Wonderland*, is a close and ingenious parody of "The Old Man's Comforts" by Robert Southey.

## CONCRETE POETRY

Concrete poems, or shape poetry, are picture poems made of letters and words. Strongly visual concrete poetry

breaks away from any and all traditional poetic forms—
poetry to be seen and felt as much as read or heard.

A classic example appears in Carroll's *Alice's Adventures in Wonderland*: When the mouse is telling Alice that his is "a long and sad *tale*" and she is looking down at him agreeing that his is indeed "a long and sad *tail*," her idea of the *tale* comes out this way:

*Fury said to a*
*mouse, That he*
*met in the*
*house,*
*"Let us*
*both go to*
*law: I will*
*prosecute*
*you. Come,*
*I'll take no*
*denial; We*
*must have a*
*trial: For*
*really this*
*morning I've*
*nothing*
*to do."*
*Said the*

*mouse to the*
*cur, "Such*
*a trial,*
*dear Sir,*
*With*
*no jury*
*or judge,*
*would be*
*wasting*
*our*
*breath."*
*"I'll be*
*judge, I'll*
*be jury,"*
*said*
*cunning*
*old Fury:*
*"I'll*
*try the*
*whole*
*cause*
*and*
*condemn*
*you*
*to*
*death!"*

In the early 1970s several volumes of concrete poetry for children became popular. Ian Hamilton Finlay, a Scottish artist, established his own small press, printing many of his concrete poems in books and on posters and postcards. Poetry from his best-known title, *Poems to Hear and See*, is still widely anthologized, though the book is out of print.

*Seeing Things*, written and designed by Robert Froman, with lettering by Ray Barber, consists of fifty-one selections arranged on the pages in shapes appropriate to their subjects. One clever poem entitled "Graveyard" shows ten tombstones with one lettered word on each reading: "A nice place to visit but you wouldn't live there."

More recently Joan Bransfield Graham's *Splish Splash* features twenty-one exuberant compositions in concrete poetry celebrating water in its various forms, from waterfalls to ice cubes, steam to snow. The handsomely designed volume is illustrated by Steven Scott.

## ASIAN VERSE FORMS

Over the past three decades Asian verse forms—in particular haiku, senryu, and tanka, stemming from ancient Japanese culture, and sijo from Korea—have gained wide popularity with teachers and students in all grade levels. Once the forms are introduced to students, they can be encouraged to experiment with and strive to perfect them.

## HAIKU

There are many reasons for the successful use of haiku with children—the poems are short, and the form is easy to remember and, with practice, enjoyable to construct. Invented in Japan centuries ago, haiku consists of three unrhymed lines containing seventeen syllables, five-seven-five respectively. Since the Japanese language differs from English, the number of syllables changes when original Japanese haiku are translated.

The basic requirement is that, in some way, the haiku should relate to nature or the seasons of the year. Haiku should strike an image almost as if a slide had been flashed upon a screen in a darkened room.

Children of all ages can try to create haiku, concentrating and writing about a brief moment; no child, however, should be forced initially into the five-seven-five syllable limitations. I recall receiving a letter from a Michigan fifth grader who was puzzled over "Hokku Poems" by Richard Wright in *The Poetry of Black America*, edited by Arnold Adoff, because two of the verses did not meet the "required" seventeen syllables. The required form should be suggested to students, but not rigidly enforced. The world will not be shattered if Wright's haiku, or any child's, contains eighteen syllables or fifteen! The point is to motivate children of varying ability to express themselves in a few words and decide which words can be used to communicate poetic ideas.

Before introducing the form, read to the class a variety of haiku that pinpoint the qualities desired.

Excellent examples of haiku appear in *In a Spring Garden*, edited by Richard Lewis, a collection by classic master writers of the form, including Issa, Bashō, and Buson. The text follows a spring day from the early admonition to a toad who "looks as if/It would belch forth/A cloud," to the glowing good night of a firefly. The artist Ezra Jack Keats provided vibrant collage illustrations to complement this treasure.

*Red Dragonfly on My Shoulder*, edited by Sylvia Cassedy and Kunihiro Suetake, presents thirteen haiku about animals, each set as a simple sentence on a double-page spread. Molly Bang, a two-time Caldecott Honor recipient, interprets each selection with fascinating collages using "pieces of ordinary life"—actual cookies, corn chips, clamshells, and chocolate-covered almonds that bring the words to unique heights.

*Wind in the Long Grass*, edited by William J. Higginson, culls haiku from writers around the world, illustrated with full-color paintings by Sandra Speidel.

*Spring: A Haiku Story*, edited by George Shannon, consists of fourteen selections arranged to show the delights and wonders of a spring walk. Spare in design, the book is illustrated in full-color folk-art paintings by Malcah Zeldis.

Two original collections include *Black Swan/White Crow*, by J. Patrick Lewis—thirteen haiku, each set on a double-page spread—and *Cricket Never Does*, by Myra Cohn Livingston, featuring sixty-two haiku and tanka.

*Grass Sandals: The Travels of Bashō*, by Dawnine Spivak, is a simple retelling of the story of Bashō, one of the most beloved poets in Japanese history, and his travels across his island homeland. Woven into the text are nine haiku. The book is beautifully designed and illustrated by Demi.

The adult volume *The Haiku Anthology*, edited by Cor van den Heuvel, provides countless examples to share with children of all ages. In addition to haiku written in the standard form, there are a number of short thoughts expressed in single lines, some as short as five words!

There are many volumes explaining the haiku form. Published in 1967, the compact paperbound volume *Haiku in English* by Harold G. Henderson is still one of best guides. Henderson cites many examples of haiku by master poets and suggests sound lesson plans. The volume is one that every teacher should have, ready to be pulled out at a second's notice.

To motivate a lesson in writing haiku, I brought a bunch of jonquils into a fifth-grade class and placed them in a clear vase filled with water. Alongside the vase I placed a Mason jar containing a live bumblebee, caught by one of the students in my class—not by me! This was done prior to the morning admission bell. Several children, upon entering the classroom, noticed the fresh flowers and the bee on my desk. Other children came in and went to their desks without bothering to look at my display. Soon, however, there was more buzzing in the classroom than any swarm of healthy bees could have produced. When the entire class settled, I asked them to look at, concentrate on, the flowers and the bumblebee for just three minutes, which can be a long, long time for thirty curious creators. I told them to look at the flowers and the bee as they had never looked at anything before.

At the end of three minutes I carried the jar to the window, dramatically opened it, and sent Mr. Bumblebee off to freedom. I then asked the class to think about the entire experience—the flowers, the bottled-up bee, and my letting it go free. I had provided them with nature, a moment, and an image.

Frieda wrote:

*The bee is set free*
*But flowers, you'll only stay*
*Alive for a while.*

Harriet created:

*Yellow bee, go to*
*The yellow flowers outside*
*Where you both are free.*

Many simple objects from nature might be used to stimulate youngsters—a twig, a rock, a cricket, or a bunch of leaves. With our continued emphasis on ecology, haiku is a natural tie-in between language arts and science. Many haiku written by great masters centuries ago are perhaps more relevant today than they might have been at the time they were written.

## SENRYU

Senryu, another popular verse form related to haiku, was named after Karai Hachiemon, an eighteenth-century government official in the Asakusa district of Edo (now

Tokyo), who wrote under the pen name Senryu, meaning River Willow. Ironically, Senryu never wrote in the form named after him!

Senryu follows the same five-seven-five pattern of haiku and also concentrates on a single idea or image of a moment. The form differs in that the subject matter is not restricted to nature or the seasons. This form gives students the opportunity to express ideas on any subject—everyday happenings from playing baseball to eating pizza or camping out in the woods. A second grader created:

*The first day of school.*
*Now I know that butterflies*
*Can be in bellies.*

*Senryu: Poems of the People*, by J. C. Brown, is a small treasure of verse containing work dating from the eighteenth to the early twentieth centuries.

## TANKA

Tanka are longer in form than haiku and senryu and typically deal with nature or a season of the year. Tanka is written in five lines totaling thirty-one syllables, five-seven-five-seven-seven respectively. The first three lines are known as the *hokku*; the last two, the *ageku*. Most children find it more satisfying to experiment with the tanka form after they have been introduced to and practiced haiku. Examples of tanka can found in *Cricket Never Does* by Myra Cohn Livingston.

Each January in Tokyo a poetry party is held at the Imperial Palace, where writers are invited to read their tanka poems while millions of people view the fete on television. Poetry ceremonies at the Imperial Palace date back to the tenth century.

## SIJO

The Korean verse form sijo is a product of the four-teenth-century Yi dynasty, a period in Korean history during which science, industry, literature, and the arts developed rapidly.

The form, similar to haiku in several ways, is based on syllabication, is unrhymed, and usually deals with nature or the seasons. In English the form is often written in six lines, each line containing seven or eight syllables with a total of forty-two to forty-eight syllables. Orginally, sijo verse was written to be sung while accompanied by a lute or while the rhythm was beaten on a drum.

One hot summer day, while working with a group of students in Hartford, Connecticut, I introduced the sijo form. When I asked what they might like to write about, two replies came simultaneously: "Somethin' cold," said one child; another replied, "Old Man Winter!" Thus, thoughts of winter were conjured up in sijo form while we all melted away. One child produced:

*Winter is a God-given gift*
*It's a pretty good one, too!*

*To see the white flakes falling*
*And cold, cold winds a-blowin'*
*Life seems like the seasons*
*Changing with no reasons.*

A boy in the group wrote:

*What a gloomy, snowy night.*
*Dull, moody, all the way.*
*The ship's crew are all in fright . . .*
*The choppy waves roll off the coast . . .*
*In the galley, pots are rattling.*
*Storm-stopped ships on their way.*

In Harlem, New York, a sixth-grade unit on Korea
incorporated the sijo form into language arts programs.
One boy wrote:

*I wonder what it's like to*
*Be a crawling caterpillar.*
*They're always so alone*
*And ugly and without friends, and sad . . .*
*But when the time comes*
*Everyone is fooled—a butterfly is born!*

In the examples above you will note that the seven-
to-eight-syllable count per line does vary now and then.

Each of the above forms—haiku, senryo, tanka, and
sijo—allows children to spontaneously put forth thoughts
and feelings in a minimum number of words and lines.

It must be emphasized, however, that students' writing should not necessarily have to conform to formula; overstepping the structured boundaries often enables girls and boys to write more freely.

Through short verse forms a child can play on a city street, bask in the beauty of the countryside, or even go to Neverland Land, as it was called by a child in Julesburg, Colorado.

## REFERENCES

Adoff, Arnold, editor. *The Poetry of Black America: Anthology of the 20th Century.* Harper, 1973.

Brown, J. C. *Senryu: Poems of the People.* Tuttle, 1991.

Carroll, Lewis. *Alice's Adventures in Wonderland.* Illustrated by John Tenniel. Morrow, 1992.

——. *Through the Looking Glass, and What Alice Found There.* Illustrated by John Tenniel. Morrow, 1993.

Cassedy, Sylvia, and Kunihiro Suetake, translators. *Red Dragonfly on My Shoulder.* Illustrated by Molly Bang. Harper, 1992.

Ciardi, John. *The Man Who Sang the Sillies.* Illustrated by Edward Gorey. Lippincott, 1961; also in paperback.

Crapsey, Adelaide. *Verse.* Manas Press, 1915.

Finlay, Ian Hamilton. *Poems to Hear and See.* Macmillan, 1971.

Froman, Robert. *Seeing Things: A Book of Poems.* Crowell, 1974.

Graham, Joan Bransfield. *Splish Splash.* Illustrated by Steven Scott. Ticknor and Fields, 1994.

Heard, Georgia. *For the Good of the Earth and Sun: Teaching*

*Poetry.* Heinemann, 1989; also in paperback.

Henderson, Harold G. *Haiku in English.* Tuttle, 1967.

Higginson, William J. *Wind in the Long Grass: A Collection of Haiku.* Illustrated by Sandra Speidel. Simon & Schuster, 1991.

Hoberman, Mary Ann. *A Fine Fat Pig, and Other Animal Poems.* Illustrated by Malcah Zeldis. Harper, 1991.

Juster, Norton. *As: A Surfeit of Similes.* Illustrated by David Small. Morrow, 1989.

Kennedy, X. J. *Uncle Switch: Loony Limericks.* Illustrated by John O'Brien. McElderry, 1997.

—— and Dorothy M. Kennedy, editors. *Knock at a Star: A Child's Introduction to Poetry.* Illustrated by Karen Ann Weinhaus. Little, Brown, 1982; also in paperback.

Kuskin, Karla. *Thoughts, Pictures, and Words.* Owen, 1995.

Lear, Edward. *How Pleasant to Know Mr. Lear!: Edward Lear's Selected Works.* Edited by Myra Cohn Livingston. Holiday House, 1984.

Lewis, J. Patrick. *Black Swan/White Crow: Haiku.* Illustrated by Chris Manson. Atheneum, 1995.

Lewis, Richard, editor. *In a Spring Garden.* Illustrated by Ezra Jack Keats. Dial, 1965; also in paper-back.

Livingston, Myra Cohn. *Cricket Never Does: A Collection of Haiku and Tanka.* Illustrated by Kees de Kiefte. McElderry, 1997.

——. *Poem-Making: Ways to Begin Writing Poetry.* Harper, 1991.

——. *Sky Songs.* Illustrated by Leonard Everett Fisher. Holiday House, 1984.

——, editor. *Lots of Limericks.* Illustrated by Rebecca Perry. McElderry, 1991.

Lobel, Arnold. *The Book of Pigericks: Pig Limericks.* Harper, 1983; also in paperback.

McClure, Amy A. *Sunrises and Songs: Reading and Writing Poetry in an Elementary Classroom.* Heinemann, 1990; also in paperback.

McCord, David. *One at a Time: His Collected Poems for the Young.* Illustrated by Henry B. Kane. Little, Brown, 1974.

Merriam, Eve. *The Inner City Mother Goose.* Illustrated by David Diaz. Simon & Schuster, 1996.

Sandburg, Carl. *The Complete Poems of Carl Sandburg.* Harcourt, 1970.

Shannon, George, selector. *Spring: A Haiku Story.* Illustrated by Malcah Zeldis. Greenwillow, 1996.

Spivak, Dawnine. *Grass Sandals: The Travels of Bashō.* Illustrated by Demi. Atheneum, 1997.

van den Heuvel, Cor, editor. *The Haiku Anthology: Over 700 of the Best English Language Haiku, Senryu and Related Works.* Simon & Schuster, 1986; also in paperback.

Worth, Valerie. *All the Small Poems.* Illustrated by Natalie Babbitt. Farrar, Straus, 1987; also in paperback.

# PART FOUR

# From Acorns to Zinnias

## A POTPOURRI OF POETRY IDEAS

Ideas for motivating both the study and appreciation of poetry in classrooms, libraries, and homes are offered in this section. No attempt has been made to assign age levels to these projects; they can be, and have been, used effectively as is or adapted to fit any age group. A variety of themes and approaches ties in with children's interests and school curricula.

None of the projects require excessive time or unusual materials. With a little bit of imagination and inexpensive items that can be purchased in a local novelty store, you will find that girls and boys will be passing the poetry often with pride and pleasure.

## MOTHER GOOSE
## GROWS AND GROWS

As well as being an important part of our literary heritage, Mother Goose rhymes serve as an excellent introduction to poetry. The powerful rhythm and highly imaginative, action-filled use of words, the wit, ideas, and compact structures of the rhymes, aid children in developing a lifelong interest and appreciation of verse.

Why does Mother Goose have such wide appeal to generation after generation of children? Stop and listen to the rhymes. See how they awaken responsiveness in boys and girls. They are short, fun-filled, dramatic, pleasing to the ear, easy to remember—and oh, so hard to forget.

There are many explanations as to who the real Mother Goose was. Scholars differ.

One of the best reference books on the rhymes of yore is *The Annotated Mother Goose*, edited by William Baring-Gould and Ceil Baring-Gould; this 350-page volume contains rhymes with scholarly explanations and black-and-white illustrations by such artists as Kate Greenaway, Randolph Caldecott, and Walter Crane, along with historical woodcuts.

Glorious collections of Mother Goose rhymes abound—from the 1955 Caldecott Honor Book *Book of Nursery and Mother Goose Rhymes*, edited and illustrated by Marguerite de Angeli, containing 376 rhymes with more than 260 full-color illustrations, to the fun-filled, oversized *My Very First Mother Goose*, selected by Iona Opie and delightfully illustrated by Rosemary Wells.

Many other popular artists have illustrated Mother Goose rhymes. A trip to a library or bookstore will supply countless collections.

*Mother Goose*, a multimedia program I created, contains four thematic collections in several print formats—little books, big books, and large-sized posters, as well as audiocassettes and theme resource folders. The four themes are "Mother Goose and Her Children," "Mother Goose and Her Animal Friends," "Mother Goose Through the Seasons," and "Mother Goose Around the World."

After children are familiar with a variety of Mother Goose collections, begin planning a Mother Goose village. Ask children which rhymes they would like to dramatize, what costumes, props, and scenery will be needed. Once the projects have been chosen, the village can be mapped out. Street signs such as "Jack Horner's Corner" or "King Cole's Court" can be made by children and placed around the room to show the locations of the various projects.

The entrance to the children's room of your library or to your classroom can become a giant shoe. Let children help decide what measurements are needed for the shoe; sketch an outline of it, and the doorway, on a large piece of brown wrapping paper for students to paint and cut out. After the shoe is framed around the doorway, it can be decorated with a photograph of each student—the inhabitants and stars of the Mother Goose Village. A sign reading "Welcome to Mother Goose Village" will provide a final touch.

For Contrary Mary's garden, paper flowers created

by children can be attached to sticks and planted in Styrofoam-filled shoe boxes set "all in a row" and decorated with green crepe-paper borders.

A large, rectangular cardboard box can easily serve as Humpty Dumpty's wall. Children can draw or paint bricks on the box, and Humpty can be fashioned from a large balloon. Paint on facial features with a felt-tip pen. Use cellophane tape to add a hat and a paper necktie, and then tape Humpty to the wall to await his fate. When the moment for the great fall comes, a child can pierce the balloon with a pin. Be sure to have an extra balloon on hand as an understudy, just in case Humpty explodes before his cue!

A white horse for the Lady of Banbury Cross and a cockhorse for her visitor can be made from a broom. A paper-bag horse face can cover the straw. Rags, crepe paper, or colored yarns can be tied around the end of the stick to make a tail.

Which Mother Goose rhymes take place in the country? In the city? Two backdrops can be planned to provide extra space for performers. A "rural mural" can include a haystack for Little Boy Blue, a meadow, a barn for the cow, and so on. A "city mural" might include some of the shops mentioned in the rhymes.

There are many ways to dramatize Mother Goose rhymes. Some can be recited by one child or a chorus; others can be sung by children using traditional music or their own melodies. Jane Yolen's *Mother Goose Songbook* can be especially helpful in planning a musical Mother Goose program. It includes more than forty-five rhymes accompanied by Adam Stemple's arrangements for piano and guitar. Yolen prefaces each piece with intriguing background notes.

The abilities and needs of children and the rhymes themselves will dictate the most appropriate form of dramatization. Short, familiar rhymes such as "Jack and Jill," "Little Miss Muffet," or "Humpty Dumpty" are easy to pantomime as the audience guesses the name of the rhyme presented.

Longer narrative rhymes such as "Old Mother Hubbard," or rhymes that can be expanded such as "Tom, Tom, the Piper's Son," can be enacted with puppets. For "Old Mother Hubbard" one child might narrate while others re-create the action and improvise dialogue for puppet characters.

Mother Goose rhymes can be extended as well as re-created. Consider, for example, the following based on "Hey Diddle Diddle." The cow is leaving for the moon. Present at the countdown are the Cat and the Fiddle, the Dish and the Spoon, and other animals and objects invented by the children, who can don paper-bag masks. What are the reactions of the citizens of Mother Goose Village? Will the cow make it? Live interviews can also be successful with such characters as Little Jumping Joan and the Queen of Hearts.

A first-grade class in Harlem, New York, produced

"Mother Goose Comes to New York City," in which they created their own parodies based on the rhymes. As noted, Mother Goose is effective with young children. However, she transcends ages. A third-grade class in Virginia staged a Mother Goose festival; a sixth-grade class in New Jersey held an extraordinary Mother Goose pageant, enjoyed by the entire school in the assembly hall.

Mother Goose rhymes are full of lost or missing things—lost sheep, mittens, mouse tails. There are also many things that might be missing—Jack Horner's plum or Miss Muffet's spider, for instance. Children can draw missing objects, or you can write the words for them on a piece of paper. These can then be placed in a coffee can or a cardboard well made from a milk carton. Each child can fish out a slip of paper and match the object with the Mother Goose character who lost it. Other children might prefer writing lost-and-found ads— for example, "Lost—24 blackbirds. Last seen in the King's backyard."

Many foods are mentioned in the rhymes. A class- room Mother Goose market could advertise and sell curds and whey, hot cross buns, and pease porridge hot and cold—with reduced prices for the "nine-day-old" variety! Children can make signs listing items and prices as well as for things out of stock, such as "Sorry—No Bones Today." Discount coupons can be designed for old and "new" products—for example, "Ten cents off the

Pieman's Prize Pies," or "New, Improved Microwavable Tarts! Twenty cents off."

What are some jobs mentioned in the rhymes? Do any exist today? What are they called? In a job-hunting game set at a modern employment agency, boys and girls can apply for jobs as cobblers or pie sellers. Can jobs be found to match their skills?

Little Mouse sat on a ———. Young poets can write original rhymes, perhaps creating Mother Goose–type verses about their favorite television or cartoon characters.

To enhance mathematics lessons, ask students to note rhymes containing numbers, encouraging them to make up individual word problems for classmates to solve. For example: How many men went to sea in a bowl? (Three). Add that number to the number of bags of wool the black sheep had. What is the answer? (Six). With numberless rhymes children can have great fun studying various illustrators' interpretations. For example, how many silver bells and cockleshells can be found in this picture of Contrary Mary's garden? How many in that one? How many children live in each version of the old woman's shoe?

Visual literary skills are enhanced as well when students look at and compare various illustrators' interpretations of Mother Goose characters. A child might be asked, "Which picture of Little Miss Muffet and the spider that sat down beside her is your favorite? Why?"

A last suggestion as a culminating activity for a

Mother Goose program: A picture map can be assembled from drawings of the various areas of the Mother Goose Village. The finished map can be placed on a program sheet and distributed to visitors as a memento of the village. Map skills can be reinforced by asking: "How can we get from one area of the village to another? What places do we have to pass? What is the best route?"

## ANIMAL ROUNDUP TIME

A corner of a classroom, a library, or even a child's bedroom can be set up for Animal Roundup Time. Hang a mobile from the ceiling featuring pictures of animals. A large box under the mobile can hold books of poems about animals together with models of animals children might wish to display.

Several volumes tie in well with an Animal Roundup.

You might consider: *Voices from the Wild* by David Bouchard, an unusual collection describing how twenty-five birds and animals use their senses to survive in the world. The elongated format features extraordinary paintings by Ron Parker; an informative appendix about each creature appears.

A long-time favorite, *Prayers from the Ark* by Carmen Bernos de Gasztold, translated by Rumer Godden, was first published under the titles *Le Mieux Aimé* and *Prières dans l'Arche* in the 1940s and 1950s. The first American edition, containing twenty-seven verses, appeared in 1962. A new edition featuring thirteen selections was published in 1992 with striking full-color paintings by Barry Moser. If possible, try finding the 1962 edition. You won't want to miss the fourteen poems that appear there, among which are "The Prayer of the Little Ducks," "The Prayer of the Foal," and the poignant "The Prayer of the Old Horse."

Barbara Juster Esbensen's *Words with Wrinkled Knees* contains twenty-one verses expressing the essence of the animal each identifies. The elephant, for example, trumpets "its own wide name through its nose!"—while the giraffe has a "neck so long/it has never seen its knees."

J. Patrick Lewis's *A Hippopotamusn't*, a feast of wordplay, contains thirty-five humorous works. Twenty-eight more animal antics appear in his *Two-Legged, Four-Legged, No-Legged Rhymes*.

*Advice for a Frog* by Alice Schertle offers fourteen inventive works about unusual creatures, such as the black rhinoceros on the edge of extinction and the proboscis monkey, the best swimmer among the primates, found on the island of Borneo. A brief appendix provides notes on each subject.

Schertle pays tribute to cows in fifteen serious and comic verses in *How Now, Brown Cow?*

In Marilyn Singer's *Turtle in July* there are verses about a different animal for each month of the year, such as "January Deer," "March Bear," and "Beavers in November."

Noted anthologies contain a host of animal verses too. Some outstanding titles include *Animals, Animals,* poems selected by Laura Whipple, illustrated with lush, full-color collage illustrations by Eric Carle. An "Index of Animals Alphabetically Arranged"—from Ant to Yak—will steer readers to animal poems of their choice.

The section "Mostly Animals" in *Sing a Song of Popcorn*, edited by Beatrice Schenk de Regniers and others, has twenty-seven selections illustrated in full color by Arnold Lobel.

Two collections I edited, *Side by Side* and *Surprises*, feature tributes to the animal world. In *Side by Side* the section "Birds and Beasts" contains eight works illustrated in full color by Hilary Knight; in *Surprises* the section "Who to Pet" consists of six verses illustrated by Megan Lloyd.

More than two hundred poems by 123 poets are represented in *The Beauty of the Beast*, selected by Jack Prelutsky.

Birds are well represented in Paul Fleischman's *I Am Phoenix*, a collection of poems to be read aloud by two voices; *On the Wing*, by Douglas Florian, is a light-hearted look at twenty-one birds; *Bird Watch* by Jane Yolen captures the character and personality of various members of the bird world and the seasons that surround them; Myra Cohn Livingston pays tribute to owls in her rich anthology *If the Owl Calls Again*.

Fish are the subject of *In the Swim*, Douglas Florian's book of zany light verse about underwater creatures including catfish, flying fish, and rainbow trout.

Dinosaurs? What child can resist the great beasts of yore—those fascinating creatures that disappeared from the earth sixty-five million years ago? Librarians attest that the "dinosaur shelf" is rarely full! Since girls and boys are hooked on dinosaurs, why not share some light verse and poetry about them?

Jack Prelutsky has penned his own wry look at the creatures in *Tyrannosaurus Was a Beast*. A contents page gives brief information on such creatures as Leptopterygius, Corythosaurus, and Quetzalcoatlus.

Jane Yolen offers seventeen witty ditties in *Dinosaur Dances*. "Dinosaur Hard Rock Band," "Dinosaur Waltz," and "Disco Dinosaur Dancing" are among the offerings.

*Dinosaurs*, an anthology I assembled, brings a serious view of the species to young readers. The volume begins where the dinosaurs are today—in museums—following them from their evolution to extinction. Among the varied poets contributing to *Dinosaurs* are Lilian Moore, Myra Cohn Livingston, and Valerie Worth.

Pets are a part of many children's lives. Set up a pet shop by encouraging children to share stuffed toys or, under supervision, a live pet. Children can find poems, or create original verses, to honor favorite pets.

*Raining Cats and Dogs* by Jane Yolen offers readers nine poems about cats and dogs in an upside-down-book format.

Horses are the subject of Patricia Hubble's *A Grass Green Gallop* and Nancy Springer's *Music of Their*

*Hooves*. Both volumes celebrate the beauty and motion of horses from newborn foals to wild stallions, thoroughbreds, and old cart horses.

Owners of pet mice will enjoy *Adam Mouse's Book of Poems* by Lilian Moore. It is based on the author's delightful novels *I'll Meet You at the Cucumbers* and *Don't Be Afraid, Amanda*, which skillfully blend poems written by Adam, a country mouse, to his friend Amanda, who lives in the city.

A rich gathering of twenty-five poems appears in Nancy Larrick's *Mice Are Nice* by poets such as Aileen Fisher, John Ciardi, Karla Kuskin, and Valerie Worth.

## BEST POEM
## OF THE MONTH

At the beginning of each month encourage students to find poems characteristic of that month. In February, for example, children might find poems entitled "February," or discover poems about Lincoln's Birthday, Valentine's Day, or George Washington's Birthday, or find a poem by an African American to commemorate Black History Month. Refer to "Holiday Happenings in Poetry" in this part of the volume for resources.

Set aside time for children to read aloud poems they have found, telling why each was chosen. The poems can be written out and tacked onto a bulletin board or featured on a hanging display.

During the last week of the month children can

vote on the Best Poem of the Month and select several runners-up. The winners can be kept in a poetry file to serve as a good place for students to find favorite poems to read again and again.

In one Texas classroom a teacher stretched a clothesline across the back of the room. When the children brought in poems relating to special events—holidays, children's birthdays, local events—they were placed on the clothesline and labeled with specific dates. General poems about the month, such as seasonal pieces, were also attached to the line.

Another teacher using this technique held a poetry festival at the end of the month. Each of the poems selected by the class was again read aloud—but this time to another class. Children practiced their selections; several acted them out; others used simple props for the poetry reading; some did projects to accompany the poems.

## CHORAL SPEAKING

Choral speaking is an activity that can contribute to the appreciation and enjoyment of poetry as well as provide worthwhile learning and listening experiences.

The easiest form of choral speaking involves the refrain. After hearing a poem several times, children quickly realize that the refrain appears over and over, and they eagerly await their cue to chime in on that line.

I have used, for example, Shel Silverstein's "Peanut

Butter Sandwich" in *Where the Sidewalk Ends* with boys and girls in preschool and kindergarten classes. Each of the twelve stanzas ends with the words "peanut butter sandwich." Before reading the selection, I ask them to shout out the three words. I next tell them that when I raise my hand, this is the cue for them all to shout "peanut butter sandwich." They have never failed me.

A second type of choral speaking is two-part speaking. Two groups of children say aloud various lines of the poem. An example is the traditional verse:

If You Ever Ever Ever Meet a Whale

| | |
|---|---|
| *If you ever ever ever ever ever* | ALL |
| *If you ever ever ever meet a whale* | BOYS |
| *You must never never never never touch its tail* | ALL |
| *For if you ever ever ever ever ever* | GIRLS |
| *If you ever ever ever touch its tail* | BOYS |
| *You will never never never never never* | ALL |
| *You will never never meet another whale.* | GIRLS |

Line-a-child arrangements can be somewhat difficult because of the necessity for precision of delivery. However, such readings can be satisfying because they give children a chance to speak one or more lines alone. An example:

The Squirrel

| | |
|---|---|
| *Whisky, frisky* | ALL |
| *Hippety, hop!* | ALL |

| | |
|---|---|
| *Up he goes* | SOLO |
| *To the treetop!* | |
| *Whirly, twirly,* | ALL |
| *Round and round!* | |
| *Down he scampers* | SOLO |
| *To the ground.* | |
| *Furly, curly.* | SOLO |
| *What a tail!* | SOLO |
| *Tall as a feather,* | SOLO |
| *Broad as a sail!* | SOLO |
| *Where's his supper?* | ALL |
| *In the shell,* | SOLO |
| *Snap, cracky,* | ALL |
| *Out it fell!* | SOLO |

The most difficult type of choral speech is unison speaking, for it involves all students speaking at the same time. Perfect timing, balance, phrasing, inflection, and pronunciation are required, which takes much practice and preparation time.

Two readers can read aloud alternately, one taking the left-hand part, the other taking the right-hand part, meshing together to create a duet.

In two of his books, *I Am Phoenix* and *Joyful Noise*, Paul Fleischman offers choral speaking using two voices. *I Am Phoenix* contains fifteen selections about bird life; *Joyful Noise* features fourteen verses about the insect world.

Programs of choral speaking can be enhanced by lighting effects and interesting staging techniques, such as grouping children in semicircles, scattering them around the stage, or interspersing simple dance and mime with their readings.

Choral speaking helps develop good speech, provides the timid child with a degree of self-confidence, and gives many pleasurable moments.

## CITY SONGS

For those who live in a city, the sights, sounds, and smells can evoke a multitude of imagery. For children who live in rural or suburban areas, you might ask if any of them have visited a city. A list of city sights (subways, street vendors, skyscrapers, etc.) can be prepared and discussed to motivate children to write poems about urban life.

One of the earliest books of poetry to reflect urban life is the classic *Bronzeville Boys and Girls* by Gwendolyn Brooks, published in 1956. Since that date other volumes have steadily appeared to capture the vitality and excitement, the problems and pleasures, of living in a city.

*Street Music* by Arnold Adoff celebrates the varied

people and rhythms of a city—from pedestrians who crowd the streets to honking taxis in a traffic jam to a symphony of music along city streets that vibrate "hot metal" language combinations.

*Night on Neighborhood Street* by Eloise Greenfield introduces readers to urban African-American families, friends, and neighbors.

*"C" Is for City* by Nikki Grimes is a book of alphabet rhymes, from ads for apartments to "zillions of churches named Zion." Large, full-color paintings by Pat Cummings are packed with alphabetical items for readers to search for. There is a key in the back of the book in case the reader misses anything.

A collection I wrote, *Good Rhymes, Good Times!*, begins with "Sing a Song of Cities." Urban settings—a museum, brownstones, delicatessens, fire escapes—are brought to life via Frané Lessac's full-color illustrations.

Part Six of X. J. Kennedy's *The Forgetful Wishing Well* contains eight selections touching on various aspects of cities, including "Boulder, Colorado," "Forty-Seventh Street Crash," "Flying Uptown Backwards," "How to Watch Statues," and "Roofscape."

*Bam Bam Bam* by Eve Merriam, about a wrecking ball that demolishes old houses and stores to make way for a skyscraper, is vibrantly illustrated with graphics by Dan Yaccarino.

Jane Yolen's anthology *Sky Scrape/City Scape* has

twenty-five poems by such favorite poets as Myra Cohn Livingston, Eve Merriam, and Lilian Moore, as well as newer voices.

## COLOR ME POETRY

There are a number of successful ways to involve children in finding or writing poems about color. A bright array of colored wrapping tissue on a bulletin board, with the caption "Find a Poem About Me," could provide the inspiration a child might need to write about colors.

A dramatic technique for stimulating girls and boys to think about color is to use an overhead projector. Place a clear bowl filled with water atop the projector—a plastic turtle bowl or a clear glass pie plate works best. By dropping a few drops of food coloring into the bowl, you can make magical things happen on a screen. The coloring can be stirred around or blown to create movements, or colors can be mixed together to produce new color combinations.

In a kindergarten class viewing this procedure, one boy remarked, "Oh, my! The water's starting to bleed!"

Paint blots are useful in writing poetry about color. Children can drip large drops of tempera paint on construction paper and carefully fold the paper in half. When it is opened, they will find an interesting paint blot, à la Rorschach. Titles can be given to their creations, and appropriate poems that best illustrate their blots can be found or written.

In *Hailstones and Halibut Bones* by Mary O'Neill, twelve verses about various colors appear, each asking a question: "What Is Gold?" "What Is Orange?" "What Is Red?" The poems not only tell about the colors of objects but touch upon the way color can make us feel—for example: "Orange is brave/Orange is bold"; "Gold is feeling/Like a king"; "Blue is feeling/Sad or low."

The poems stir our senses, make us want to look around carefully to see everyday colors we take for granted and see them anew in fresh, poetic imagery. First published in 1961, the volume was reissued in 1989, with new illustrations by John Wallner.

To further encourage children to create color images, make available to them specific objects—a zinnia, some colored leaves, a black ant; their physical presence will awaken mental images.

*Greens* by Arnold Adoff also provides children with insights about color.

A Las Vegas, Nevada, teacher asks her students to describe thoughts about color not often written about. She poses, "How do certain colors make you feel?" Several responses include:

*Aqua makes me feel like a mermaid dancing in the sea.*

*Bronze makes me feel like a dead statue.*

*Amber makes me feel like millions of waves of grain.*

Color is all around and about us. Use it to broaden children's writing.

### FOOD POEMS TO
### SATISFY YOUNG APPETITES

On a bulletin board post the question "What's for Lunch?" A table setting can be depicted by stapling a paper tablecloth onto the bulletin board for a background, along with paper plates, cups, and plastic cutlery. The latter can be mounted with double-faced masking or cellophane tape, strong glue, or Velcro.

A food poem appears on each plate. One might describe eating an ice cream cone on a hot summer's day, another the spicy taste of chili con carne or relishes on a hot dog. Before lunch might be a good time to read a selection from the plates.

Poems dealing with food are offered in *Eats* and *Chocolate Dreams* by Arnold Adoff. *Eats* includes poetic morsels on Chinese food, spaghetti, and apple pie. *Chocolate Dreams* is Adoff's tribute to his favorite flavor.

Several anthologies contain a host of food poems.

William Cole's anthology *Poem Stew* offers a feast of funny verses on such subjects as the creased prune and rhinoceros stew. The poems are written by Kaye Starbird, Richard Armour, and others, and include six by Cole himself.

Bobbye S. Goldstein's *What's on the Menu?* includes work by John Ciardi, X. J. Kennedy, and Dorothy Aldis.

*Food Fight*, edited and illustrated by Michael J.

Rosen, was compiled to aid Share Our Strength, the nation's leading antihunger organization. This rich collection offers thirty-three never-before-published poems by such notable poets as Nikki Grimes, Jack Prelutsky, and Paul Fleischman.

## HAPPY BIRTHDAY, DEAR POET

Being introduced to poets and their work can be stimulating for children. Use a bulletin board and tabletop display to highlight a particular poet of the month. The bulletin board can feature biographical information along with several of the poet's poems printed on oaktag. If possible, include a photograph of the poet. A table display can feature volumes of the poet's work and, if available, a recording of his or her voice or that of another person reading from the poet's work.

Each day a selection or two from the featured books can be read aloud and/or recordings can be listened to. Encourage children to look for additional biographical information on the poet or to seek out more examples of his or her work.

The poets and their birthdays listed below suggest choices for your students' poet-of-the-month celebrations:

JANUARY
6 Carl Sandburg
13 N. M. Bodecker
18 A. A. Milne

FEBRUARY
    1 Langston Hughes
    2 Judith Viorst
    11 Jane Yolen
    13 Eleanor Farjeon

MARCH
    2 Dr. Seuss
    17 Lilian Moore
    26 Robert Frost
    28 Byrd Baylor

APRIL
    13 Lee Bennett Hopkins
    22 William Jay Smith
    26 William Shakespeare

MAY
    5 J. Patrick Lewis
    12 Edward Lear
    17 Eloise Greenfield
    25 Theodore Roethke
    31 Elizabeth Coatsworth

JUNE
    6 Nancy Willard
    7 Gwendolyn Brooks
      Nikki Giovanni
    24 John Ciardi
    26 Charlotte Zolotow
    27 Lucille Clifton

JULY
10 Rebecca Kai Dotlich
16 Arnold Adoff
17 Karla Kuskin
19 Eve Merriam

AUGUST
16 Beatrice Schenk de Regniers
17 Myra Cohn Livingston
19 Ogden Nash
21 X. J. Kennedy

SEPTEMBER
8 Jack Prelutsky
9 Aileen Fisher
25 Harry Behn
26 T. S. Eliot

OCTOBER
14 e. e. cummings
20 Nikki Grimes
27 Lillian Morrison
29 Valerie Worth

NOVEMBER
13 Robert Louis Stevenson
15 David McCord

DECEMBER
5 Christina G. Rossetti
10 Emily Dickinson

## HOLIDAY HAPPENINGS
## IN POETRY

Holidays hold a special place in all our hearts. Thanksgiving, inherited from the Pilgrims, connects us with our early history and customs; Easter and Christmas are joyous days that are shared with people the world over; St. Valentine's Day and Halloween, though not considered legal holidays, bring to us hundreds of years of culture, custom, wit and wisdom, folklore—and fun!

Poetry about these and other major and minor holidays abounds. Here is a Holiday Book Calendar citing books you can share with children of all ages.

### VALENTINE'S DAY

*Good Morning to You, Valentine*, selected by Lee
    Bennett Hopkins
*Valentine Poems*, selected by Myra Cohn
    Livingston
*It's Valentine's Day*, by Jack Prelutsky

### EASTER

*Easter Buds Are Springing*, selected by Lee
    Bennett Hopkins

### HALLOWEEN

*Hey-How for Halloween!*, selected by Lee Bennett
    Hopkins
*Halloween A B C*, by Eve Merriam
*It's Halloween*, by Jack Prelutsky
*Best Witches*, by Jane Yolen

Although not specifically Halloween in theme, *Nightmares* and *The Headless Horseman Rides Tonight* by Jack Prelutsky will spook readers.

*The Three Bears Holiday Rhyme Book*, by Jane Yolen, contains poems about several holidays.

Through such collections readers will meet works by "old-timers" such as William Shakespeare and Joyce Kilmer; they'll find the contemporary voices of Aileen Fisher and Lilian Moore; and they'll weave in and out of old-new voices, too—poets who have been read by generation after generation of children and still speak strongly to us today—including such treasured poets as Langston Hughes, Carl Sandburg, Dorothy Aldis, and David McCord.

Holiday celebrations can be enhanced when girls and boys design their own greeting cards. Appropriate poems can be selected for cards or original poems written, illustrated, and sent on such occasions as birthdays and Mother's or Father's Day—ideal times to share poetic thoughts with relatives and special friends.

## JUST THINGS

Common, everyday objects all take on new meaning via the poet's crystal vision. There are poems written about almost anything under the sun and even verses about things beyond the sun—literally! From *a*pples to *z*ebras—and in between—black holes and bubbles, pizzas and pincushions, quasars and quilts, spaghetti and starfish are all topics that poets have addressed.

A rich source of poetry about a variety of things is Valerie Worth's *All the Small Poems and Fourteen More*, 113 verses about topics from *a*corns to *z*innias. Incredible metaphors characterize Worth's creations—sharp, clear views of objects such as fleas and fireworks, coins and Christmas lights, asparagus and raw carrots.

To encourage students to think, read, and write about everyday objects, I have taken groups on a spontaneous "pick-me-up" walk. I ask each child to pick something up during our walk—a leaf, a pebble, a discarded can, a paper clip—anything they might spot. Next, the children are given time to observe these objects and find a poem written about them or create their own work.

Another activity centered around "just things" is offered by Melissa Cain, a literature consultant in Perrysburg, Ohio. She suggests gathering together a box full of items and wrapping them individually in tissue paper. The students each choose something from the box to unwrap. They may keep it or trade it for something another student has, then use the item as the subject of a poem "to make their object extraordinary through an original piece of writing." Both the objects and the poems can be used for a library or classroom display.

Other poetry collections that deal with "things" are: *Ordinary Things* by Ralph Fletcher (an arrowhead, letter, mailboxes, railroad tracks); *The Great Frog Race* by Kristine O'Connell George (a metal bucket, plowed fields, a monkey wrench); *Keepers* by Alice Schertle (a carousel, a dinosaur bone, a ukulele); *Small Talk*, an anthology I compiled including such poems as "Fog" by J. Patrick Lewis, "Fossils" by Rebecca Kai Dotlich, and "Wet Socks" by James Hayford.

## MAPPING POETRY

Poetry reflects people, their lifestyles, experiences, dreams, feelings, ideals, and ideas. Reading what poets from all over the world have to say, children can better understand how all people are alike and yet different.

Beginning with the United States, post a map of America on a bulletin board. Underneath it set up a table display of books featuring poetry. In addition to place names or origins highlighted in the poems, children can research the part of the country where their favorite poets live or lived. Often this information is found on book jackets. As children's repertoires grow, they will begin to see that poets come from all walks of life and environs. Some leading American poets they will encounter are Karla Kuskin, New York and Virginia; Gwendolyn Brooks, Illinois; Aileen Fisher, Colorado; Eloise Greenfield, Washington, D.C.

Anthologies are rich resources to highlight Americana. *The Oxford Book of Children's Verse in America*, edited by Donald Hall, begins with psalms and highlights work from Michael Wigglesworth (1631–1705) through to Jack Prelutsky (1940– ). Each poet is represented by one or more selections. "Appended Notes" on the poets are an added bonus.

*Hand in Hand*, a poetry collection I edited, is a sweeping panorama of American history from colonial times to the future. The book, divided into nine sections, is illustrated with Peter Fiore's watercolor paintings.

*Celebrate America in Poetry and Art*, edited by Nora Panzer, celebrates in poetry two hundred years of "life and history." The five sections are illustrated with paintings, drawings, photographs of sculpture, and other works of art culled from the the Smithsonian Institution's National Museum of American Art.

*Singing America*, edited by Neil Philip, is rich in work by Emily Dickinson, Edna St. Vincent Millay, and Walt Whitman, as well as traditional spirituals, anthems, and North American songs. Dramatic black-and-white drawings by Michael McCurdy illustrate the volume.

Moving past the United States, young readers will find a wealth of Caribbean poetry available to them.

A map showing the location of various Caribbean islands can highlight poems and help children gain insight about this colorful environment, its people, and its landscapes.

Eloise Greenfield's *Under the Sunday Tree* contains twenty poems with vivid, full-color impressionistic paintings by Mr. Amos Ferguson.

In *Coconut Kind of Day* Lynn Joseph offers thirteen poems glowingly illustrated in full color by Sandra Speidel.

Monica Gunning, born in Jamaica, shows both the hardships and the joyous adventures of a Caribbean childhood in *Not a Copper Penny in Me House*, strikingly illustrated by Frané Lessac, and in *Under the Breadfruit Tree*, with stark illustrations by Fabricio Vanden Broeck.

Older readers can delight in *When I Dance* by James Berry, which contains a number of Caribbean celebrations in verse, from "Sunny Market Song" to a bevy of "Jamaican Caribbean Proverbs."

Anthologies provide varied voices from Caribbean roots.

*A Caribbean Dozen*, edited by John Agard and Grace Nichols, introduces thirteen poets who preface their work with memories of childhood experiences. A variety of art techniques by Cathie Felstead illustrates the book.

Trinidad-born Grace Hallworth includes more than twenty playground folk rhymes in *Down by the River*, an oversized book containing exuberant paintings by Caroline Binch.

*Caribbean Canvas*, edited by Frané Lessac—who lived on the little island of Montserrat in the Lesser Antilles—offers a dozen poems and proverbs via a pictorial journey of island life.

To highlight poetry from other continents, a world map will be helpful in pinpointing various countries and cultures along with a book display that might include the following titles:

*The Distant Talking Drum* by a native of Nigeria,

Isaac Olaleye, describes life and customs in a Nigerian village through fifteen poems, illustrated by Frané Lessac. "A Walk Through My Rain Forest" is a perfect verse for a study of this incredible natural phenomenon.

China is represented in *Maples in the Mist*, translated by Minfong Ho. The poems traditionally taught to Chinese children come from the Tang Dynasty (A.D. 618–907), a time in which the arts and poetry in China flourished. Illustrations are by Taiwan-born artists Jean and Mou-sien Tseng.

Chinese lore is also represented in *Chinese Mother Goose Rhymes*, selected by Robert Wyndham. Designed to be read vertically, Chinese calligraphy ornaments the margins of each page. Forty traditional rhymes, riddles, lullabies, and games that have amused Chinese children for generations are included. Full-color illustrations by Ed Young decorate the pages.

*O Jerusalem* by Jane Yolen celebrates the three-thousand-year history of the holy place for three major religions—Judaism, Christianity, and Islam. Fourteen poems along with notes are illustrated by John Thompson.

*My Mexico = México Mío* by Tony Johnston brings the spirit of the country via eighteen poems in both English and Spanish, with illustrations by F. John Sierra.

In *The Tree Is Older Than You Are* Naomi Shihab Nye gathers the work of sixty-four Mexican poets and painters; Spanish-language poems and their English translations are placed side by side.

Nye's *This Same Sky* is an anthology that showcases 129 poets from sixty-eight countries celebrating the natural world and its human and animal inhabitants. "Notes on the Contributors" and a world map are appended.

Two volumes of Latin American songs and rhyme selected and illustrated by Puerto Rican–born Lulu Delacre are *Arroz Con Leche* and *Las Navidades*. *Arroz Con Leche* features a dozen songs and rhymes; *Las Navidades* is a feast of thirteen popular songs and rhymes arranged chronologically from Christmas Eve to Epiphany. Both books are printed in Spanish alongside English translations with appended musical scores.

Students might prepare a poetry atlas featuring poems from continent to continent, illustrating it with original drawings and appropriate sections cut from world maps.

## A PICTURE FOR A POEM/ A POEM FOR A PICTURE

Post an interesting photograph or print where children can easily see it. They can hunt for poems they feel fit the mood or describe the illustration. Catchy titles add to such displays; for example, the caption "Sneak into This Haunted House," under an illustration of an old house—the "hauntier" the better—might elicit original poems or a poem such as "The Haunted House" in *Nightmares* by Jack Prelutsky.

Other pictures and captions might depict nature, the

environment, space, sports, or the sea.

Stephanie J. Bissell, a first-grade teacher at Silver-thorne Elementary School in Silverthorne, Colorado, uses a similar idea to tie poetry to art appreciation. One artist is featured per month—for example, Georgia O'Keeffe, Vincent van Gogh, or Edward Hopper. Poetry sought and shared relates in theme with selected paintings. Van Gogh's painting *Rain* is paired with Langston Hughes' "April Rain Song" from *The Dream Keeper*.

Mary Schenk, an eighth-grade teacher in Bronxville, New York, and Joanna Goodman, a visiting poet, provided their students with reproductions of paintings by artists such as Pablo Picasso, Salvador Dalí, and René Magritte. Students were asked how they would feel if they were inside various paintings. Sharing works by well-known poets encouraged students to write their own poetry about the paintings. An incredible culmination of this project occurred when the educators contacted the National Gallery in Washington, D.C., and the gallery administrators agreed to hang several of the poems in its bookstore.

Try a variation of this idea by encouraging boys and girls to draw or paint a picture and then find a poem that relates to it. Several children can look for poems they feel appropriate for a classmate's drawing. If they cannot find a suitable poem, they may decide to write their own. In any case, children will have looked at a variety of poems, and the next time they paint, they may remember just the right verse to accompany their pictures.

## POETRY HAPPENINGS

Students can plan poetry happenings or a dramatic reading of several poems relating to a specific subject. Poems can tie in with curriculum, specific interests such as sports or hobbies, or a subject—rocks, the city, famous people, or music. When they have a final selection, students can present a poetry happening for their class and for other classes in their school. To enhance the happening, simple props or creative dramatics can be employed.

On a school visit in Westchester County, New York, I was dazzled by a fourth-grade production based on my collection *Song and Dance.*

One group dramatized "Rappers" by Chetra E. Kotzas, using choral speaking, setting it against a taped rap-music background. Poems, indeed, popped throughout the room! Another group did a similar enactment for "What Is Jazz?" by Mary O'Neill. The entire class rousingly performed "Birds' Square Dance" by Beverly McLoughland, with lavish paper-bag masks they made to represent the various birds mentioned in the verse, along with taped music. Two children took Carl Sandburg's "Lines Written for Gene Kelly to Dance to," using voice, mime, and strains of "Singin' in the Rain" to bring the verse to new life. Other selections were dramatized with the use of simple staging techniques—children moving about on stools and a stepladder enhanced by a spotlight.

To see and hear the performance was pure magic. The finale, a group rendition of Rebecca Kai Dotlich's "Nightdance," where "All over the world/there are night-dance children . . . " brought the thespians a hooting, standing ovation—while sending shivers up and down *my* spine.

Any grouping of poems lends itself to a multitude of production ideas. Try it!

## PROSE AND POETRY

Prose and poetry go well together. After children have read a favorite book or listened to one read aloud, follow it up with a poem. For example, if you share *The Snowy Day* by Ezra Jack Keats, you can add depth to the moment with the poem "Cynthia in the Snow" by Gwendolyn Brooks in *Bronzeville Boys and Girls*. This enables children to see and listen to a Caldecott Award–winning volume and hear a poem by a Pulitzer Prize–winning poet—all tucked into a ten- or fifteen-minute time period.

This combined approach to prose and poetry works well with older children. After reading a novel, a more mature reader can look for a poem reflecting the book's subject or theme. For example, after reading a Marguerite Henry or Walter Farley novel about horses, the reader can look for a poem about horses. A story such as *The Mouse and the Motorcycle* by Beverly Cleary is sure to send all those who like rodents scurrying for a poem expressing feelings about mice, such as those in Nancy Larrick's collection *Mice Are Nice*.

Nonfiction can be dealt with in the same way. After boys and girls have a read a book about dinosaurs or space travel, encourage them to look for a dinosaur or space poem to share.

Misha Arenstein, a fourth-grade teacher in Scarsdale, New York, uses this technique for book sharing: He asks students to tuck a poem related to a book inside the cover so that when others read it, they already have a poem on hand to read, too. He then encourages readers to add another poem. Within months one novel might have three, four, or more verses relating to the plot, characters, or setting inside its cover for future readers to enjoy.

Another way to spark the use of poetry along with prose is by encouraging children to read or reread favorite fairy tales and introduce them to humorous verses about characters, plots, or situations. After discussing the plot of "Cinderella," for instance, children will howl over ". . . And Then the Prince Knelt Down and Tried to Put the Glass Slipper on Cinderella's Foot" by Judith Viorst, from *If I Were in Charge of the World and Other Worries*. It briefly relates how Cinderella has changed her mind about the handsome prince the day after the ball. The same readers of the fairy tale will also enjoy the irreverent "Cinderella" in Roald Dahl's *Revolting Rhymes*.

## SENSES AND POETRY

Children can create poems after they have had a variety of planned sensory experiences. For example, take children on several walks around the community. Be specific about the goal of each walk. Tell young walkers, "Today we are going on a *hearing* walk. We will write down the various sounds we hear." On a second walk children can record all that they see; on a third, all they smell, and so on.

A second-grade class visited a nearby pond for a "seeing" walk. The children were fascinated by the many seedpods that appeared on a bank of the pond. Bringing some pods back into the classroom, several students wrote:

*Seedpods when they break look like bombs exploding.*

*Seedpods sail like parachutes when they open.*

*The pods look like cotton candy when they are put together.*

*I could eat it, but I won't.*

A third-grade teacher in Indianapolis, Indiana, asks her class to listen to nature through imaginative questions. She asks: "How does a brook sound?" "What song does a cricket sing?" "What tool do you think of when you hear a woodpecker?" "How do raindrops sound against your umbrella?"

Sounds can arouse young writers. To inspire creative

writing, suggest that children record a variety of every-day sounds—bacon frying, the ticking of a clock, a slam-ming door, a baby crying, an electric razor buzzing. After doing so, a fourth-grade class in Harlem, New York, composed:

Noise
*Noise, noise everywhere*
*What to do! It's always there.*
*Bang! Pow! Zoom! Crunch!*
*Buzz! Crack! Crack! Munch!*

*In the air, on the ground,*
*Noise, noise all around.*
*Dogs barking, cars parking,*
*Planes flying, babies crying.*

*Sh . . . sh . . . time for sleep.*
*Not a single little peep.*
*Oh, no—through the door—*
*Comes a noisy, awful snore.*

*Tick-tock—stop the clock.*
*Stop the yelling on my block.*
*Close the windows, shut them tight.*
*Cotton in ear—nighty-night.*

Suzanne Hunsucker, a teacher in Riverton High School in Wyoming, offers this idea for "sensational writing":

*I bombarded [the children's] senses as they walked into the classroom. . . . Music was playing, crepe paper hanging. I passed out chocolate kisses and small pieces of material to feel, and I sprayed the air with spice room deodorizer. All this launched a good discussion of the senses. . . .*

*To develop the sense of touch, we blindfolded some volunteers and had them describe objects they were feeling without actually naming them. For sound, we wrote thoughts to music and tape-recorded sounds. For development of sight, I first prepared a slide show of famous paintings and described how to look for such elements as shape, design, perspective, texture, movement, lighting, and color. Students began to really look at and analyze these works with a critical eye. . . .*

After children have had such sensory experiences, they can be encouraged to look for or write poems that deal with the senses.

*Ordinary Things: Poems from a Walk in Early Spring* by Ralph Fletcher is a book to awaken senses.

## WEATHER

Younger boys and girls can learn to keep a poetry weather calendar. Use a large piece of oaktag for each month. List the month, weeks, and days of the week, along with the question "What is the weather like today?"

To the bottom of the chart attach several large brown envelopes labeled "Sun Poems," "Wind Poems," "Cloud

Poems," "Rain Poems," or "Snow Poems." Collected verses can be placed within the appropriate envelopes. After each month, date, and day of the week is discussed, a child volunteer can describe the day's weather, choose a poem, and read it aloud. Weather combinations such as "sunny and windy" can also be used.

Girls and boys can be encouraged to add to the envelopes as they find various weather poems throughout the year.

Caroline Feller Bauer's collections of stories and a host of poems appear in *Rainy Day*, *Snowy Day*, and *Windy Day*. Large type and attractive layouts make for inviting reading.

Two further suggestions for poetry on weather are a collection I edited, *Weather*, and Jane Yolen's *Weather Report*.

## WHAT IS POETRY?

In addition to the many quotes about poetry that appear throughout this volume, the following can be used as inspiration for a variety of occasions or shared with students to evoke discussion:

*Poetry is the most effective way of saying things.*
    —Matthew Arnold.

*You may not shout when you remember poems you have read or learned, but you will know from your toes to your head that something has hit you.*
    —Arna Bontemps

*Poetry is beautiful shorthand.*

—William Cole

*Poetry makes possible the deepest kind of personal possession of the world.*

—James Dickey

*If I read a book and it makes my whole body so cold that no fire can ever warm me, I know that is poetry. If I feel physically as if the top of my head were taken off, I know that is poetry. These are the only ways I know it is. Is there another way?*

—Emily Dickinson

*A poem . . . begins as a lump in the throat, a sense of wrong, a homesickness, a lovesickness.*

—Robert Frost

*Poetry is comment on the world by people who see the world more clearly than other people and are moved by it.*

—Phyllis McGinley

*Poetry is speaking painting.*

—Plutarch

*Poetry is a record of the best and happiest moments of the happiest and best minds.*

—Percy Bysshe Shelley

## POETRY-PEDIA

In addition to the aforementioned, here is a list of ten general subjects, citing volumes of poetry to use with children of all ages.

### FAMILY FARE

Hoberman, Mary Ann. *Fathers, Mothers, Sisters, Brothers*
Hopkins, Lee Bennett, editor. "Families, Families" in
    *Worlds of Poetry*
Livingston, Myra Cohn. *There Was a Place*
———, editor. *Poems for Brothers, Poems for Sisters*
———. *Poems for Grandmothers*
Steptoe, Javaka. *In Daddy's Arms I Am Tall*
Strickland, Dorothy S., and Michael R., editors. *Families*

### FRIENDS

Katz, Bobbi. *Could We Be Friends?*
Livingston, Myra Cohn, editor. *I Like You, If You Like Me*
Mavor, Salley, editor. *You and Me*

### MATHEMATICS

Hopkins, Lee Bennett, editor. *Marvelous Math*

### MUSIC AND DANCE

Engvick, William, editor. *Lullabies and Night Songs*
Esbensen, Barbara Juster. *Dance With Me*
Hopkins, Lee Bennett, editor. *Song and Dance*
Strickland, Michael R., editor. *My Own Song*
———. *Poems to Sing to You*

## SCHOOL LIFE

Dakos, Kalli. *Don't Read This Book, Whatever You Do*
——. *The Goof Who Invented Homework*
——. *If You're Not Here, Please Raise Your Hand*
——. *Mrs. Cole on an Onion Roll*
Hopkins, Lee Bennett. *School Supplies*
Kennedy, Dorothy M., editor. *I Thought I'd Take My Rat to School*
Shields, Carol Diggory. *Lunch Money*
Singer, Marilyn. *All We Needed to Say*
Winters, Kay. *Did You See What I Saw?*

## SEA SONGS

Livingston, Myra Cohn. *Sea Songs*
Shaw, Alison, editor. *Until I Saw the Sea*
Yolen, Jane. *Sea Watch*

## SEASONS

Esbensen, Barbara Juster. *Cold Stars and Fireflies*
Frank, Josette, editor. *Snow Toward Evening*
Hopkins, Lee Bennett, editor. *Side by Side*
Kennedy, X. J. *The Kite That Braved Old Orchard Beach*
Livingston, Myra Cohn. *A Circle of Seasons*
Rogasky, Barbara, editor. *Winter Poems*
Updike, John. *A Child's Calendar*
Yolen, Jane. *Ring of Earth*
——, editor. *Once Upon Ice*

## SPACE

Hopkins, Lee Bennett, editor. *Blast Off!*
Livingston, Myra Cohn. *Space Songs*
Simon, Seymour, editor. *Star Walk*

## SPORTS

Adoff, Arnold. *Sports Pages*

Greenfield, Eloise. *For the Love of the Game: Michael Jordan and Me*

Hopkins, Lee Bennett, editor. *Extra Innings*

——. *Opening Days*

——. *Sports! Sports! Sports!*

Janeczko, Paul. *That Sweet Diamond*

Knudson, R. R., and May Swenson, editors. *American Sports Poems*

Mathis, Sharon Bell. *Red Dog/Blue Fly*

Morrison, Lillian, editor. *At the Crack of the Bat*

——. *Slam Dunk*

## TREES

Behn, Harry. *Trees*

Brenner, Barbara, editor. *The Earth Is Painted Green*

Livingston, Myra Cohn. *Monkey Puzzle*

## REFERENCES

Adoff, Arnold. *Chocolate Dreams: Poems.* Illustrated by Turi MacCombie. Lothrop, 1989.

——. *Eats: Poems.* Illustrated by Susan Russo. Lothrop, 1979; also in paperback.

——. *Greens: Poems.* Illustrated by Betsy Lewin. Lothrop, 1988.

——. *Sports Pages.* Illustrated by Steve Kuzma. Harper, 1986; also in paperback.

——. *Street Music: City Poems.* Illustrated by Karen Barbour. Harper, 1995.

Agard, John, and Grace Nichols, editors. *A Caribbean*

*Dozen: Poems from Caribbean Poets.* Illustrated by Cathie
Felstead. Candlewick, 1994.

Baring-Gould, William S., and Ceil Baring-Gould, editors.
*The Annotated Mother Goose: Nursery Rhymes Old and
New.* Clarkson Potter, 1982.

Bauer, Caroline Feller, editor. *Rainy Day: Stories and Poems.*
Illustrated by Michele Chessare. Lippincott, 1986.

——. *Snowy Day: Stories and Poems.* Illustrated by Margot
Tomes. Lippincott, 1986; also in paperback.

——. *Windy Day: Stories and Poems.* Illustrated by Dirk
Zimmer. Lippincott, 1988.

Behn, Harry. *Trees: A Poem.* Illustrated by James Endicott.
Henry Holt, 1992.

Bernos de Gasztold, Carmen. *Prayers from the Ark: Selected
Poems.* Translated by Rumer Godden. Illustrated by
Jean Primose. Viking, 1962; new selected edition illustrated by Barry Moser, Viking, 1992; also in paperback.

Berry, James. *When I Dance.* Illustrated by Karen Barbour.
Harcourt, 1991.

Bouchard, David. *Voices from the Wild: An Animal
Sensagoria.* Illustrated by Ron Parker. Chronicle, 1996.

Brenner, Barbara, editor. *The Earth Is Painted Green: A
Garden of Poems About Our Planet.* Illustrated by
S. D. Schindler. Scholastic, 1994.

Brooks, Gwendolyn. *Bronzeville Boys and Girls.* Illustrated by
Ronni Solbert. Harper, 1956.

Cleary, Beverly. *The Mouse and the Motorcycle.* Illustrated by
Louis Darling. Morrow, 1965; also in paperback.

Cole, William, editor. *Poem Stew.* Illustrated by Karen Ann
Weinhaus. Lippincott, 1981; also in paperback.

Dahl, Roald. *Revolting Rhymes*. Illustrated by Quentin Blake. Knopf, 1982; also in paperback.

Dakos, Kalli. *Don't Read This Book Whatever You Do: More Poems About School*. Illustrated by G. Brian Karas. Four Winds, 1993.

——. *The Goof Who Invented Homework and Other School Poems*. Illustrated by Denise Brunkus. Dial, 1996.

——. *If You're Not Here, Please Raise Your Hand: Poems About School*. Illustrated by G. Brian Karas. Simon & Schuster, 1990; also in paperback.

——. *Mrs. Cole on an Onion Roll, and Other School Poems*. Illustrated by JoAnn Adinolfi. Simon & Schuster, 1995.

de Angeli, Marguerite, editor. *Book of Nursery and Mother Goose Rhymes*. Doubleday, 1954.

Delacre, Lulu, selector. *Arroz Con Leche: Popular Songs and Rhymes from Latin America*. Scholastic, 1989.

——. *Las Navidades: Popular Christmas Songs from Latin America*. Scholastic, 1990.

de Regniers, Beatrice Schenk, and others, editors. *Sing a Song of Popcorn: Every Child's Book of Poems*. Illustrated by Marcia Brown, Leo and Diane Dillon, Richard Egielski, Trina Schart Hyman, Arnold Lobel, Maurice Sendak, Marc Simont, Margot Zemach. Scholastic, 1988.

Eliot, T. S. *Old Possum's Book of Practical Cats*. Illustrated by Edward Gorey. Harcourt, 1982; revised edition; also in paperback.

Engvick, William, editor. *Lullabies and Night Songs*. Music by Alec Wilder. Illustrated by Maurice Sendak. Harper, 1965.

Esbensen, Barbara Juster. *Cold Stars and Fireflies: Poems of the Four Seasons.* Illustrated by Susan Bonners. Crowell, 1984.

——. *Dance With Me.* Illustrated by Megan Lloyd. Harper, 1995.

——. *Words With Wrinkled Knees: Animal Poems.* Illustrated by John Stadler. Crowell, 1986; reissued by Boyds Mills, 1997.

Fleischman, Paul. *I Am Phoenix: Poems for Two Voices.* Illustrated by Ken Nutt. Harper, 1985; also in paperback.

——. *Joyful Noise: Poems for Two Voices.* Illustrated by Eric Beddows. Harper, 1988; also in paperback.

Fletcher, Ralph. *Ordinary Things: Poems from a Walk in Early Spring.* Atheneum, 1997.

Florian, Douglas. *In the Swim: Poems and Paintings.* Harcourt, 1997.

——. *On the Wing: Bird Poems and Paintings.* Harcourt, 1996.

Frank, Josette, editor. *Snow Toward Evening: A Year in a River Valley: Nature Poems.* Illustrated by Thomas Locker. Dial, 1990; also in paperback.

George, Kristine O'Connell. *The Great Frog Race and Other Poems.* Illustrated by Kate Kiesler. Clarion, 1997.

Goldstein, Bobbye S., editor. *What's on the Menu?: Food Poems.* Illustrated by Chris Demarest. Viking, 1992.

Greenfield, Eloise. *For the Love of the Game: Michael Jordan and Me.* Illustrated by Jan Spivey Gilchrist. Harper, 1997.

——. *Night on Neigborhood Street.* Illustrated by Jan Spivey Gilchrist. Dial, 1991.

——. *Under the Sunday Tree.* Illustrated by Mr. Amos

Ferguson. Harper, 1988; also in paperback.

Grimes, Nikki. *C Is for City*. Illustrated by Pat Cummings. Lothrop, 1995.

Gunning, Monica. *Not a Copper Penny in Me House: Poems from the Caribbean*. Illustrated by Frané Lessac. Boyds Mills, 1993.

——. *Under the Breadfruit Tree: Island Poems*. Illustrated by Fabricio Vanden Broek. Boyds Mills, 1998.

Hall, Donald, editor. *The Oxford Book of Children's Verse in America*. Oxford University Press, 1985; also in paperback.

Hallworth, Grace, editor. *Down by the River: Afro-Caribbean Rhymes, Games, and Songs for Children*. Illustrated by Caroline Binch. Scholastic, 1996.

Ho, Minfong, editor and translator. *Maples in the Mist: Children's Poems from the Tang Dynasty*. Illustrated by Jean and Mou-sien Tseng. Lothrop, 1996.

Hoberman, Mary Ann. *Fathers, Mothers, Sisters, Brothers: A Collection of Family Poems*. Illustrated by Marylin Hafner. Joy Street, 1991; also in paperback.

Hopkins, Lee Bennett. *Good Rhymes, Good Times*. Illustrated by Frané Lessac. Harper, 1995.

——, editor. *Blast Off!: Poems About Space*. Illustrated by Melissa Sweet. Harper, 1995; also in paperback.

——. *Dinosaurs: Poems*. Illustrated by Murray Tinkelman. Harcourt, 1987; also in paperback.

——. *Extra Innings: Baseball Poems*. Illustrated by Scott Medlock. Harcourt, 1993.

—. *Easter Buds Are Springing: Poems for Easter*. Illustrated by Tomie de Paola. Boyds Mills, 1979.

——. *Good Morning to You, Valentine: Poems*. Illustrated by

Tomie de Paola. Harcourt, 1976; Boyds Mills, 1991.

———. *Hand in Hand: An American History Through Poetry.* Illustrated by Peter M. Fiore. Simon & Schuster, 1994.

———. *Hey-How for Halloween!* Illustrated by Janet McCaffery. Harcourt, 1974.

———. *Marvelous Math: A Book of Poems.* Illustrated by Karen Barbour. Simon & Schuster, 1997.

———. *Mother Goose.* William H. Sadlier, Inc., 1998.

———. *Opening Days: Sports Poems.* Illustrated by Scott Medlock. Harcourt, 1996.

———. *School Supplies: A Book of Poems.* Illustrated by Renée Flower. Simon & Schuster, 1996.

———. *Side by Side: Poems to Read Together.* Illustrated by Hilary Knight. Simon & Schuster, 1988; also in paperback.

———. *Small Talk: A Book of Short Poems.* Illustrated by Susan Gaber. Harcourt, 1995.

———. *Song and Dance: Poems.* Illustrated by Cheryl Munro Taylor. Simon & Schuster, 1997.

———. *Sports! Sports! Sports!: A Poetry Collection.* Illustrated by Brian Floca. Harper, 1999.

———. *Surprises.* Illustrated by Megan Lloyd. Harper, 1984; also in paperback.

———. *Weather.* Illustrated by Melanie Hall. Harper, 1994; also in paperback.

———. *Worlds of Poetry.* William H. Sadlier, Inc., 1998.

Hubbell, Patricia. *A Grass Green Gallop: Poems.* Illustrated by Ronald Himler. Atheneum, 1990.

Hughes, Langston. *The Dream Keeper and Other Poems.* Illustrated by Brian Pinkney. Knopf, 1994.

Janeczko, Paul. *That Sweet Diamond: Baseball Poems.*

Illustrated by Carole Katchen. Atheneum, 1998.

Johnston, Tony. *My Mexico = México Mío*. Illustrated by F. John Sierra. Putnam, 1996.

Joseph, Lynn. *Coconut Kind of Day: Island Poems*. Illustrated by Sandra Speidel. Lothrop, 1990; also in paperback.

Katz, Bobbi. *Could We Be Friends?: Poems for Pals*. Illustrated by Joung Un Kim. Mondo, 1997.

Keats, Ezra Jack. *The Snowy Day*. Viking, 1962; also in paperback.

Kennedy, Dorothy M., editor. *I Thought I'd Take My Rat to School: Poems for September to June*. Illustrated by Abby Castas. Little, Brown, 1993.

Kennedy, X. J. *The Forgetful Wishing Well: Poems for Young People*. Illustrated by Monica Incisa. Atheneum, 1985.

———. *The Kite That Braved Old Orchard Beach: Year-Round Poems for Young People*. Illustrated by Marian Young. McElderry, 1991.

Knudson, R. R., and May Swenson, editors. *American Sports Poems*. Orchard, 1988.

Larrick, Nancy, editor. *Mice Are Nice*. Illustrated by Ed Young. Putnam, 1990.

Lessac, Frané, editor. *Caribbean Canvas*. Boyds Mills, 1994.

Lewis, J. Patrick. *A Hippopotamusn't and Other Animal Verses*. Illustrated by Victoria Chess. Dial, 1990; also in paperback.

Livingston, Myra Cohn. *Birthday Poems*. Illustrated by Margot Tomes. Holiday House, 1989.

———. *A Circle of Seasons*. Illustrated by Leonard Everett Fisher. Holiday House, 1982; also in paperback.

———. *Monkey Puzzle and Other Poems*. Illustrated by Antonio Frasconi. Atheneum, 1984.

——. *Sea Songs*. Illustrated by Leonard Everett Fisher. Holiday House, 1986.

——. *Space Songs*. Illustrated by Leonard Everett Fisher. Holiday House, 1988.

——. *There Was a Place and Other Poems*. McElderry, 1988.

——, editor. *If The Owl Calls Again: A Collection of Owl Poems*. Illustrated by Antonio Frasconi. Atheneum, 1990.

——. *I Like You, If You Like Me: Poems of Friendship*. McElderry Books, 1987.

——. *Poems for Brothers, Poems for Sisters*. Illustrated by Jean Zallinger. Holiday House, 1991.

——. *Poems for Grandmothers*. Illustrated by Patricia Cullen-Clark. Holiday House, 1990.

——. *Valentine Poems*. Illustrated by Patience Brewster. Holiday House, 1987.

Mathis, Sharon Bell. *Red Dog, Blue Fly: Football Poems*. Illustrated by Jan Spivey Gilchrist. Viking, 1991; also in paperback.

Mavor, Salley, editor. *You and Me: Poems of Friendship*. Orchard, 1997.

McCord, David. *One at a Time: His Collected Poems for the Young*. Illustrated by Henry B. Kane. Little, Brown, 1977.

Merriam, Eve. *Bam Bam Bam*. Illustrated by Dan Yaccarino. Henry Holt, 1995.

——. *Halloween A B C*. Illustrated by Lane Smith. Macmillan, 1987; also in paperback.

Moore, Lilian. *Adam Mouse's Book of Poems*. Illustrated by Kathleen Garry McCord. Atheneum, 1992.

———. *Don't Be Afraid, Amanda.* Illustrated by Kathleen Garry McCord. Atheneum, 1992.

———. *I'll Meet You at the Cucumbers.* Illustrated by Sharon Woodling. Atheneum, 1988.

Morrison, Lillian, editor. *At the Crack of the Bat: Baseball Poems.* Illustrated by Steve Cieslawski. Hyperion, 1992; also in paperback.

———. *Slam Dunk: Basketball Poems.* Illustrated by Bill James. Hyperion, 1995; also in paperback.

Nye, Naomi Shihab, editor. *This Same Sky: A Collection of Poems from Around the World.* Four Winds, 1992; also in paperback.

———. *The Tree Is Older Than You Are: A Bilingual Gathering of Poems and Stories from Mexico.* Simon & Schuster, 1995; also in paperback.

Olaleye, Isaac. *The Distant Talking Drum: Poems from Nigeria.* Illustrated by Frané Lessac. Wordsong/Boyds Mills, 1995.

O'Neill, Mary. *Hailstones and Halibut Bones: Adventures in Color.* Illustrated by John Wallner. Doubleday, 1961.

Opie, Iona, editor. *My Very First Mother Goose.* Illustrated by Rosemary Wells. Candlewick, 1996.

Panzer, Nora, editor. *Celebrate America in Poetry and Art.* Hyperion, 1994.

Philip, Neil, editor. *Singing America.* Illustrated by Michael McCurdy. Viking, 1995.

Prelutsky, Jack. *The Headless Horseman Rides Tonight: More Poems to Trouble Your Sleep.* Illustrated by Arnold Lobel. Greenwillow, 1980; also in paperback.

———. *It's Halloween.* Illustrated by Marylin Hafner. Greenwillow, 1977.

——. *It's Valentine's Day.* Illustrated by Yossi Abolafia. Greenwillow, 1983; also in paperback.

——. *Nightmares: Poems to Trouble Your Sleep.* Illustrated by Arnold Lobel. Greenwillow, 1976; also in paperback.

——. *Tyrannosaurus Was a Beast: Dinosaur Poems.* Illustrated by Arnold Lobel. Greenwillow, 1988; also in paperback.

——, editor. *The Beauty of the Beast: Poems of the Animal Kingdom.* Illustrated by Meilo So. Random House, 1997.

Rogasky, Barbara, selector. *Winter Poems.* Illustrated by Trina Schart Hyman. Scholastic, 1994.

Rosen, Michael J., editor. *Food Fight: Poets Join the Fight Against Hunger with Poems About Their Favorite Foods.* Harcourt, 1996.

Schertle, Alice. *Advice for a Frog and Other Poems.* Illustrated by Norman Green. Lothrop, 1995.

——. *How Now, Brown Cow?* Illustrated by Amanda Schaffer. Browndeer, 1994.

——. *Keepers.* Illustrated by Ted Rand. Lothrop, 1996.

Shaw, Alison, editor. *Until I Saw the Sea: A Collection of Seashore Poems.* Henry Holt, 1995; also in paperback.

Shields, Carol Diggory. *Lunch Money and Other Poems About School.* Illustrated by Paul Meisel. Dutton, 1995; also in paperback.

Silverstein, Shel. *Where the Sidewalk Ends.* Harper, 1974.

Simon, Seymour, editor. *Star Walk.* Morrow, 1995.

Singer, Marilyn. *All We Needed to Say: Poems about School from Tanya and Sophie.* Photographs by Lorna Clark. Atheneum, 1996.

——. *Turtle in July.* Illustrated by Jerry Pinkney.

Macmillan, 1989; also in paperback.

Springer, Nancy. *Music of Their Hooves: Poems about Horses.* Illustrated by Sandy Rabinowitz. Wordsong/Boyds Mills, 1994.

Steptoe, Javaka, editor. *In Daddy's Arms I Am Tall: African Americans Celebrating Fathers.* Lee & Low, 1997.

Strickland, Dorothy S., and Michael R. Strickland, editors. *Families: Poems Celebrating the African American Experience.* Illustrated by John Ward. Boyds Mills, 1994; also in paperback.

Strickland, Michael R., editor. *My Own Song: And Other Poems to Groove to.* Illustrated by Eric Sabee. Boyds Mills, 1997.

———. *Poems that Sing to You.* Illustrated by Alan Leiner. Boyds Mills, 1993.

Updike, John. *A Child's Calendar.* Illustrated by Nancy Ekholm Burkert. Knopf, 1965.

Viorst, Judith. *If I Were in Charge of the World and Other Worries: Poems for Children and Their Parents.* Illustrated by Lynn Cherry. Atheneum, 1981; also in paperback.

Whipple, Laura, editor. *Animals, Animals.* Illustrated by Eric Carle. Philomel, 1989.

Winters, Kay. *Did You See What I Saw? Poems About School.* Illustrated by Martha Weston. Viking, 1996.

Worth, Valerie. *All the Small Poems and Fourteen More.* Illustrated by Natalie Babbitt. Farrar, Straus, 1994.

Wyndham, Robert, editor. *Chinese Mother Goose Rhymes.* Illustrated by Ed Young. Putnam, 1982; also in paperback.

Yolen, Jane. *Best Witches: Poems for Halloween.* Illustrated by Elise Primavera. Putnam, 1989.

———. *Bird Watch: A Book of Poetry.* Illustrated by Ted Lewin. Putnam, 1990.

———. *Dinosaur Dances.* Illustrated by Bruce Degen. Putnam, 1990.

———. *O Jerusalem.* Illustrated by John Thompson. Scholastic, 1996.

———. *Raining Cats and Dogs.* Illustrated by Janet Street. Harcourt, 1993.

———. *Ring of Earth: A Child's Books of Seasons.* Illustrated by John Wallner. Harcourt, 1986.

———. *Sea Watch: A Book of Poetry.* Illustrated by Ted Lewin. Philomel, 1996.

———. *Three Bears Holiday Rhyme Book, The.* Illustrated by Jane Dyer. Harcourt, 1995.

———. *Mother Goose Songbook.* Music by Adam Stemple. Illustrated by Rosekrans Hoffman. Boyds Mills, 1992.

———, editor. *Once Upon Ice and Other Frozen Poems.* Photographs by Jason Stemple. Boyds Mills, 1997.

———. *Sky Scrape/City Scape: Poems of City Life.* Illustrated by Ken Condon. Boyds Mills, 1996.

———. *Weather Report: Poems.* Illustrated by Annie Gusman. Boyds Mills, 1993.

# AFTERWORD

In 1985 I had the honor of being chosen the Children's Book Council's National Book Week Poet. The verse I created—"Good Books, Good Times!"—to fete this occasion sums up in many ways the deep feelings I have for children and their literature, for the thoughtful time educators and parents devote to bringing the best written words to our youth:

> Good Books, Good Times!
> *Good books.*
> *Good times.*
> *Good stories.*
> *Good rhymes.*
> *Good beginnings.*
> *Good ends.*
> *Good people.*
> *Good friends.*
> *Good fiction.*
> *Good facts.*
> *Good adventures.*
> *Good acts.*
> *Good stories.*
> *Good times.*

*Good books.*

Good *times.*

May each and every one of you have a life filled with "Good Books, Good Times!"—particularly *good* rhymes. Always continue to pass the poetry, *please!*

# INDEX OF AUTHORS
## AND TITLES